THE UNITED STATES OF AMERICA

Designed and Produced by
Ted Smart & David Gibbon

Text by Bill Harris

Featuring the photography of
Edmund Nägele F.R.P.S.
and Peter Beney

MAYFLOWER BOOKS · NEW YORK CITY

CONTENTS

	Page
New England	18
Mid-Atlantic States	58
Appalachian Highlands	96
The Southeast	120
Great Lake States	156
The Heartland	172
The Southwest	192
Mountain States	236
Pacific Coast States	264
Hawaii	304
Alaska	312

IN THIS TEMPLE
AS IN THE HEARTS OF THE PEOPLE
FOR WHOM HE SAVED THE UNION
THE MEMORY OF ABRAHAM LINCOLN
IS ENSHRINED FOREVER

ON a crisp day in 1977, a big jet from Europe touched down at the airport in Bangor, Maine. Erwin Kreuz, a brewery worker from West Germany, strolled into the terminal building for a sample of the local beer, which he found acceptable; then he set out to see the sights.

Maine is spectacular in October. The forests are scarlet, yellow and orange, the air is crystal clear, and though winter is on the way, Indian summer is still there. Mr Kreuz had obviously picked a perfect time to visit.

He drank it in for three days. But all the while, he had a strange feeling that something was wrong. Something was. He thought he was in San Francisco. There are no cable cars in Bangor, no Golden Gate, no China-town, no Fisherman's Wharf, no Nob Hill. They're all 3,000 miles away!

The story has a happy ending, though. They treated him like a king in Maine for a week, then packed him off to the West Coast where the party went on for another week.

His adventure is almost the story of America. Back in 1492, Christopher Columbus discovered it, but he was so sure he was someplace else, he named the natives "Indians". Columbus was out to prove the world was round, and he was certain he could reach the exotic East by sailing west, so it's obvious he thought he was in India. When he realized he wasn't, he moved on.

About 500 years before him, Norsemen led by Leif Ericson apparently stumbled on North America. They called it "Vinland The Good", but didn't think it was good enough either to stay or even make a record of their visit.

There are stories that Swedes and Norwegians came to America from Greenland in the 13th century. And still more that say America was really discovered by the Irish, or the Welsh, or the Chinese, or the Phoenicians. But through it all, none of them seems to have known what they discovered. And none of them cared.

Once it had been discovered, however, people came to explore it. And in almost every case, what they were really looking for was a way *around* it or even *through* it.

Columbus never knew he had discovered a whole new continent, but he found out enough about it to know that it was rich in gold and silver; and to the Spanish who financed his expedition, that was a whole lot better than spices from the Orient or some half-baked theory about the shape of the world. Within 20 years they were exporting a million dollars a year in gold and silver from America, and that encouraged them to look around for more.

In the process they established colonies, including St. Augustine on the Florida peninsula in 1565. It was the first permanent European settlement in the United States. So permanent, it's still there.

Meanwhile, watching Spain's wealth growing encouraged others to explore this new world. French explorers claimed all the territory from the Carolinas north to the St. Lawrence River and settled in Nova Scotia, Florida and South Carolina.

The English got into the act, too. But they found it more fun to raid the Spanish treasure ships than to build towns and farms. One of the pirates, Sir Water Raleigh, used his Spanish treasure to start a colony in Virginia. Though his original colony ultimately failed, it did succeed in introducing tobacco to the world and helped the British realize there was, perhaps, more to America than gold and silver.

In the first half of the 17th century Europeans began arriving and settling down. The English set up shop in Jamestown, Virginia, in 1607. A year later the French arrived in Quebec. Twenty years later, the Dutch founded Nieuw Amsterdam, and 10 years after that, the Swedes established a colony in Delaware. The Dutch eased them out rather quickly; then the British moved the Dutch out of their colony and renamed it New York.

While all this was going on, the French were pushing inland toward the Great Lakes and down the Mississippi to the Gulf of Mexico. The stage was set for war.

There were four wars in all, beginning with one called "King William's War", and ending with one called "The Seven Years War". Oddly enough, none was fought in America, but America was what they were all about. When they were over, France had lost claim to her American colonies, and England and Spain divided up the country between them. Under the treaty, Spain got all the territory west of the Mississippi and England claimed everything to the east.

The Spaniards thought they had made a good deal. They had found great riches among the Aztecs and Incas in Mexico and South America, and the Indians told them there were "Seven Cities of Gold" to the north. Indeed, a Spanish priest in search of heathen to convert had reported seeing one of them somewhere near where the Arizona–New Mexico border is today. They had been exploring the territory for a century, going as far north as Kansas, as far west as California. They didn't find the "Seven Cities of Gold" – no one ever has – but they were fairly certain they weren't <u>east</u> of the Mississippi.

The British were slow starters in colonizing America, but ultimately their colonies were the most successful. In 1620, just a few years after the founding of the Virginia colony, a group of religious dissenters arrived in Cape Cod Bay, Massachusetts. As Puritans, life under James I in England had been less than joyous, even to these people who considered ''joy'' a four-letter word. With the King's blessing 101 of them, and a ship's crew of 48, had set out to escape persecution and to find a new life in the New World.

Their ship, of course, was the ''Mayflower''; their colony, Plymouth, and they are remembered today as ''Pilgrims''. They were Englishmen first, travelling with the permission of the Crown and at the expense of The London Company, who owned the settlements in Virginia.

Some say they were off course, some say it was a careful plan; but the fact is, they landed far north of the Virginia colony outside the jurisdiction of The London Company. This left them free to make their own rules, and before leaving the ship they drew up a document that became the law of their colony. Basically, it bound them together to voluntarily obey the rule of the majority. It was an almost revolutionary idea in 1620, and it became the first step toward another bigger revolutionary idea, the United States Constitution.

Life was far from easy for the colonists on Cape Cod Bay, but they managed to survive in spite of it. Within 20 years, they had a thriving colony of hard-working souls. A decade later, they had absorbed more than 20,000 in the biggest mass migration England has ever seen. To make room for the newcomers, they started some new towns with such names as Cambridge, Charlestown, Gloucester and Boston.

As often happens when oppressed people look for freedom, the Massachusetts settlers didn't give much freedom to people who didn't agree with them. It wasn't long before they had dissenters among themselves, who went down the Cape to start a colony of their own, which they called Rhode Island.

The soil in Massachusetts was poor for farming, so another group set out further south and settled down in Connecticut, which made the Dutch in Nieuw Amsterdam very nervous indeed. More of them went up to the southern coast of Maine, which had already been settled by the French, and still more moved west into New Hampshire.

The Indians had been friendly, even helpful, to the colonists, but all this expansion was too much. The Puritans didn't believe in buying territory from the natives; they just marched in and took it. The tribes in Connecticut didn't think that was right, and so they rebelled by attacking the settlements. In retaliation, a force went out from Massachusetts and wiped out an entire tribe, destroying their villages and capturing survivors to sell as slaves in the West Indies. That solved their immediate problem, but gave them a much bigger one in return. And so to protect themselves from the hostile savages, the colonists bound themselves together in a confederation they called ''New England''.

Meanwhile, people were pouring into the new world from old England. The King was giving away huge tracts of land to both his creditors and his old friends. One of those friends, Sir George Calvert, had visited Virginia and liked it very much. But he wasn't allowed to stay because he was a Roman Catholic. The King fixed that by giving him land north of Virginia. Calvert died soon after, and the grant went to his son, the second Lord Baltimore, who named the estate ''Maryland'', which he established as a colony for English Catholics.

The southern and middle colonies were run almost like feudal estates. The grants decreed that any laws passed should not violate English law and should have the consent of the people. But the land owners were free to give or sell land to settlers on whatever terms they decided. Baltimore's terms were possibly the most feudal in the entire British Empire, and his colony was slow to grow. He also faced unreasonable anti-Catholicism, and finally the third Lord Baltimore was forced to convert to the Anglican Church to keep control of his grandfather's grant.

Not all the settlers in the English colonies came from England. By the time King Charles II repaid some favors by giving the Carolinas to eight of his cronies, not many Englishmen were eager to leave home. But Barbados and the other British West Indies islands had become very crowded, and some of the planters there were more than happy to migrate north and west. They brought along an institution that would become an American tradition for the next 200 years: slavery.

Once the English had convinced the Dutch that New Netherland was not a healthy place to live, the King gave the territory to his brother, the Duke of York, who in turn gave it his name. He gave the southern part of his grant to two of his friends, who called it ''New Jersey''.

They, in turn, sold part of their land to a group of Quakers, one of whom was William Penn. The land didn't have access to the ocean, so Penn approached the Duke of York, who had taken over a territory to the south on the mistaken assumption that it was part of his grant. Penn bought it from him and established a colony called ''Delaware''.

William Penn's father had been a close friend to, and creditor of, the King. Penn inherited the friendship and the unpaid dept, for which he accepted an American land grant. He set up a colony called "Pennsylvania", dedicated to complete religious freedom. Though intended as a refuge for Quakers, he welcomed anyone, and as a result, his was the fastest-growing colony America had yet seen. The Quakers came in huge numbers, along with Mennonites, Baptists, Jews and others. They came from Wales and Scotland and Ireland, from Sweden and from Germany. And they all agreed that they liked what they found there. Even the natives were friendly. Penn was fair-minded to a fault, and made it a point to pay the Indians for their land. He also made treaties that were fair to both sides and made sure that they were backed up. The result was that Pennsylvania farmers, who didn't own guns, lived in complete peace with the Indians while settlers all around them lived in terror of the "savages".

It was more than 50 years later that the last of the major English colonies was established when James Oglethorpe set up Georgia as a haven for people from the debtors' prisons in England.

Over the following 40 years, cities grew, farmers and trappers began moving further west and immigrants kept pouring in from all over Europe. By 1760, the population had reached 1,700,000, the country was prosperous and the cities cosmopolitan. A whole continent stretched out to the west waiting to be conquered. But first, the British had to be overcome.

It started quietly, of course. Most wars do. Word had gone out that the British were going to Lexington in Massachusetts to arrest a pair of rebels named Sam Adams and John Hancock. About 70 patriots, calling themselves "Minutemen", assembled on the village green to take a stand against them. And there, on April 19, 1775, a pistol shot rang out, followed by a volley of rifle fire from the British Redcoats. Within a month, Great Britain was at war with her American colonies. The war would last until 1781, when General George Washington, with the help of the French Marquis de Lafayette, defeated the British forces at Yorktown in Virginia. As the British marched away, their band played an old march, "The World Turned Upside Down". And for them it had.

For the first time, the American stars and stripes fluttered over a free and independent nation.

That flag had 13 stars; today it has 50. At the time the peace treaty that officially ended the war was signed, the United States covered 800,000 square miles from Maine to Georgia and from the Atlantic to the Mississippi. Today it covers more than 3,600,000. There were about 3 million Americans then. Today the population has grown to more than 203 million.

What is a typical American? There is really no such thing, but combining census statistics, the typical American family would seem to live in a metropolitan suburb at about the point where Wyoming, Montana and South Dakota come together. Since there are no big cities anywhere near there, one can't help being cynical about statistical evidence. But to press on ... the typical American family, according to the census, owns its own home, which is worth about $17,000 (in a metropolitan suburb!). The family is about 90 percent white, but speaks a little Spanish, looks slightly oriental and has ancestors who were pure American Indians. The man of the house is 44 years old and he's married to a woman who admits to 41. They have 2.35 children, whom they support on an income of $9,867. That makes them affluent enough to own one and a quarter automobiles.

And so on. Every American family appears to own three radios, and more Americans own a TV set than have a bathtub or a shower in their house. They're religious too. Only about 5 percent say they have no religion at all. And of the rest, 66 percent are Protestant, 26 percent are Catholic and 3 percent are Jewish. The other 5 percent are divided among just about every religion known to mankind.

People are fond of calling America a "melting pot". But in the melting process, most of the people who migrated to the United States from other countries brought a little of the old country with them. It's as common for one American to ask another what nationality he is as to ask about his astrological sign. And some of the answers are amazing. "I'm English-Irish-German and Swedish", one might say. Or the answer might be more simply, "I'm an Italian-American". During political campaigns, it's as common to hear calls for an end to such "hyphenated Americanism" as it is to hear pleas that "no American should go to bed hungry". And with rhetoric like that, it's no wonder only about half the eligible voters ever go to the polls!

But the fact is, most Americans enjoy the sense of community that comes from sharing their roots. And while many Americans do go to bed hungry, an overwhelming percentage of them are on diets, and the average family in the United States spends more on food alone than the total annual income of the average Greek family.

It's a nation of movers. Some 20 percent look for greener pastures every year, and sometimes the moving almost amounts to a mass migration. In the last 50 years, huge numbers have moved from the South to the North and thousands more have gone the other way. Farm workers have moved to the cities; city folks have moved to the suburbs, and California doesn't ever seem to stop growing.

But the more they move, the more the population centers seem to stay the same. Only about 1.5 percent of the land in the United States is taken up by cities and towns, and more than half the people live close enough to have a Sunday picnic on the shores of the Atlantic or Pacific Oceans, the Gulf of Mexico or one of the Great Lakes. It's still very much a country of wide open spaces, and even though only about a quarter of all native-born Americans still live in the state in which they were born, more than a quarter of the total population lives along the Atlantic Coast, about the same percentage that lived there a century ago.

But almost from the beginning, the pull was from the West. After the Revolution, the Spanish still controlled Florida and the land west of the Mississippi. The British had never bothered to leave Ohio, and just about everything west of the original 13 colonies was wilderness occupied by trappers and traders, Indians and a few farmers. A generation later, the United States had bought ''Louisiana'', an area that began at the Mississippi, went past Texas and stretched west into present-day Montana and Wyoming. It doubled the size of the country and opened vast opportunities for immigrants.

People began taking advantage of the opportunity in the 1820's, when German and Irish immigrants arrived in big numbers, eager for a new life and willing to take a chance on the wild frontier. People who had been born in places like Connecticut and Maryland joined them, lured by the promise of cheap land. Farmers from the already soil-exhausted South picked up stakes and went along, too. Others went in search of adventure, some went to escape debt. But most went West because it was there. It gave them a chance to start a new life, something Americans are still doing, more than 150 years later.

By the time the migration to the West gained real impetus, there were passable roads across the Appalachian Mountains. The migrants went in Conestoga wagons, in pack trains and in fancy stage coaches. Once across the mountains, the Ohio River took them into Tennessee and Kentucky ... all the way to the Mississippi, in fact, and from there up to the Great Lakes, down to the Gulf of Mexico and across into Missouri and Arkansas.

Their new homes needed to be established in hostile wilderness, populated by Indians who didn't much like seeing their homelands turned into farms and by Europeans who egged the savages on. But those who went into Ohio found signs of a very friendly man who made it his mission in life to make their lives pleasanter.

His name was John Chapman. When he died in the 1830's, the Fort Wayne, Indiana, Sentinel reported:

"Died in the neighborhood of this city, on Tuesday last, Mr. John Chapman, better known as Johnny Appleseed. The deceased was well-known throughout this region by his eccentricity, and the strange garb he usually wore. He followed the occupation of nursery-man".

Remembering Johnny Appleseed as a ''nursery-man'' is almost the same as remembering George Washington as a ''planter''. He wandered through the wilderness for more than 50 years planting apple trees as well as other fruits and medicinal plants he knew would be useful to the settlers who followed him.

He began his wanderings in Pittsburgh, after having planted orchards all the way from Massachusetts to Pennsylvania. Everyone who knew him loved him, even the Indians who were generally hostile to the white men. But even those who loved him most had to agree he cut quite a bizarre figure. They say he wore a coffee sack with holes cut in it for arms, and a stewing kettle passed for a hat. He would appear mysteriously at the door of a settler's cabin to ask for a place to spend the night. When he was welcomed inside, he always refused to sleep anywhere but on the floor and before the sun rose in the morning, he had vanished as silently as he had appeared.

Once, when the city of Mansfield, Ohio, was being attacked by Indians, Chapman ran 30 miles to the nearest fort and was back again with help in less than 24 hours. Another story about him, which may or may not be true, was that he was seen in the woods playing with a family of bear cubs while their mother watched benignly. He always walked barefoot, even in winter, and could find his way anywhere without a compass.

Deeply religious, he led an utterly selfless life. He didn't own a gun, and couldn't hurt a living thing. A legend about him says he once doused a campfire so mosquitoes wouldn't be burned to death in the flame. He wouldn't eat meat, and would never accept anything from anyone unless he could exchange it for seeds or a small tree.

When Ohio began to get too ''crowded'' for him, he moved further west into Indiana where he finally died. For years after, people on the frontier told affectionate stories about this wonderful little man. There were so many stories, in fact, that people who didn't know better began to think there had never been such a person as Johnny Appleseed.

By the time he died, more than a million people had settled in Ohio. Almost 4 million lived west of the Allegheny Mountains, and nine more states, including Illinois, Missouri and Alabama had joined the original 13.

At about the same time, President Monroe decided it was about time to get rid of some of those Indians who stood in the way of expansion. General Andrew Jackson and Indiana's Governor William Henry Harrison, each a future President, had defused the Indian menace on the frontier and a new standing army kept it that way. Now, new treaties dictated that Eastern tribes should move West ahead of the wave of immigrants. The Creeks, Cherokees, Choctaws, Chickasaws and Seminoles were all forced to walk what they called "The Trail of Tears" into what the Government called "Indian Territory".

They called it "progress". It's a thing Americans still believe in with unabashed enthusiasm. No problem is so great that "American ingenuity" can't solve it. America first discovered its courage in these people who moved West in the 19th century. They took civilization into the wilderness and made it work. Long before the century was half over, the country was well on its way, not just to the Pacific Coast, but to a position of importance in the world no country so young had a right to expect.

One of the people who originally explored the land just west of the mountains fired the imagination of would-be frontiersmen and still inspires Americans today. His name was Daniel Boone. He was a Pennsylvanian who moved to North Carolina as a boy and spent most of his life exploring Kentucky.

On his first long trip he was captured and robbed by Indians four times and after two years of hunting came back empty-handed. But he loved every minute of the adventure, and he became a master of Indian psychology as well as an enthusiastic hunter and explorer.

His tales of the wilderness encouraged a North Carolina entrepreneur to buy Kentucky and part of Tennessee from the Cherokee Indians. His stories also got him the job of mapping a road through the territory. Once into the interior, he built a town, which he modestly called "Boonesboro". Not long after, he was taken prisoner by Shawnee Indians determined to capture and destroy the settlement. But he talked them out of it and in the process so charmed them that they adopted him into their tribe, changed his name to "Big Turtle", and treated him as the son of their chief.

But all the while, he was still their prisoner.

It was several months before he escaped and got back to Boonesboro to warn his friends the Indians were coming. When they arrived, the settlers were ready for them, resolved to fight to the death to save their town.

They nearly had to. The Shawnee kept at it for two months, trying every trick in their book to destroy the settlement. But Boone knew their tricks and so none of them worked. Finally, the Indians tried to tunnel under the stockade. Boone dug a trench in their way, but they kept at it. Then a heavy rain made their tunnel collapse and the Indians went home in disgust.

He had saved his home, but Daniel Boone was never a homebody. Leaving the great "Wilderness Road" as a permanent monument, he set out to explore even more of the country. At 65, when people today think of retiring, he joined the Lewis and Clark expedition up the Missouri River and into the Oregon Territory.

He opened the way for people as tough as himself. Men and women with large families of children built cabins in the middle of the woods. They generally cleared 40 acres or so by stripping the bark from trees so they would die. Once dead, it was a simple matter to burn away the trunks and dig out the stumps. They burned the tall grass away so new grass would feed their cattle, and planted grain on the land they had cleared. Women looked after the children, of course, when they weren't cooking, churning, hoeing, spinning, chopping wood or carrying water.

Not everyone lived in the wilderness, though. Great cities were being established, too. Cincinnati, Pittsburgh and Detroit were all lusty and thriving at the beginning of the 19th century, and in a 1795 treaty, the Indians had turned over "a piece of land six miles square at the mouth of the Chickago River, emptying into the southwest end of Lake Michigan, where a fort formerly stood". In 1803 a new fort was built there to stand guard over the gateway to the Northwest Territory. Some French traders, holdovers from the days when this was French territory, lived across the river.

The fort was destroyed in the war of 1812, and yet another was built after the war was over. It was a center for the fur trade until the market dropped, and was again reborn as the City of Chicago when a canal was dug over the old portage route the French trappers had used.

New York City has an international flavor that can't be matched by any other city in the world. San Francisco has a classic charm that makes it the favorite of most Americans; Denver has a setting that makes most other cities envious, but no other city is as truly "American" as Chicago, Illinois. New York, Boston and Philadelphia were well into their second century when people began settling down along the lake shore. But this city was different. For the first time, possibly in the history of the world, builders asked <u>women</u> what sort of houses they'd like. The answer was loud and clear. They wanted porches and big bay windows and yards that went around all four sides of the house instead of the attached row houses of other cities. They got what they wanted. It was a neighborly place then and it still is.

Chicago is where modern architecture was born and where it exists at its best. It's the city of Frank Lloyd Wright and Mies ven der Rohe and the man who started it all, Louis Sullivan. Sullivan's philosophy was based on the tradition of the early builders who took the trouble to talk with the people who had to use their buildings. He didn't think a bank should look like a fortress or a factory like a tomb. In later years, his ideas would be taken to Europe and sent back as something new. But, as can be seen in the "improvements" in cities like Atlanta and Houston, the switch from "Chicago Style" to "International Style" had a very sterilizing effect on the original idea that "a building is an act".

The good news is that Chicago is alive and well. Anyone on a search for America would do well to begin there. In its early days, once the frontier had pushed that far west, it became the gateway to the Golden West. But the door swung both ways. It also became the gateway to the East and South for the ranchers and farmers from the West, and by the time the Civil War broke out, Chicago was already what Carl Sandberg later called it: "Hog butcher for the world".

When the railroads pushed West, Chicago was at the center of the activity. It still has the biggest railroad terminal in the world and the busiest airport, and it's still the gateway to the Golden West.

The territory north of Chicago: Wisconsin, Michigan, Minnesota and all the way west to Oregon, was a land of logging camps in the early days. Instead of burning out the forests as the pioneers to the south and east had done, they were at work providing the raw material to build a country.

The loggers in the Northwest, the keelboatmen on the Mississippi, the farmers and the builders were all made of tough stuff. There was hard work to be done, and they were the right people for the job. Hard work had been an American tradition right from the start, and they made it look easy.

Another quality Americans have always admired is "rugged individualism". The Yankees in New England respected it as much as their religion, and it went west along with the country.

When Indiana was still an untamed frontier, the territory between the Missouri River and the Spanish missions in California was wild, hostile, unexplored country. It was a perfect setting for the rugged individualists they called "mountain men".

It was all the rage in London and Paris in the 1820's to own soft felt hats made of beaver hair. They were as expensive as they were fashionable, and beaver pelts brought good prices. Trappers, armed with big rifles, pistols, tomahawks and hunting knives ran their lines across the plains and into the Rocky Mountains beyond. In later years, Buffalo Bill made himself the personification of these mountain men, who were the first white men to see the huge herds of buffalo on the plains, the first to ride through the Rockies, the first to fight the Apache and other hostile Indians in the West. They wore big-brimmed hats and fringed leather shirts and pants; their faces were smeared with campfire grease and their hair streamed out behind them as they rode their horses over trails only Indians had ever seen.

They lived their lives in the mountains and on the prairies, slipping back toward the east about once a year to meet traders who went out from St. Louis to meet them and to exchange beaver pelts for whiskey and fresh clothes.

Meanwhile, the Spanish hadn't given up looking for the fabled "Seven Cities of Gold", but by now they had confined their activities to the Southwest from New Mexico and across Texas into California. They had missions and settlements up the California coast from San Diego to San Francisco. And, as if they didn't have enough troubles in the desert peopled by angry Indians, the Russians were coming.

The Czar was as interested as anyone else in Europe in finding a "Northwest Passage" across North America, and he sent an explorer named Vitus Bering to take a look.

Bering explored Alaska and discovered it was rich in otter, a happy little animal whose fur was very highly-prized in China. That lured trappers from Siberia, who ranged down the coast to within about 50 miles of the Spanish settlement at San Francisco.

At the same time, British fur traders moved west across Canada. And Americans, including a New Yorker named John Jacob Astor, set up trading posts at the edge of the Oregon territory. The days of Spanish California were clearly numbered.

Back East, Americans were dreaming a new dream. Until then, the lure had been gold or timber or furs. But the American dream was for the land itself. Many of the immigrants from Europe had come from peasant stock, and the idea of actually owning their own land was almost too good to be true. They came to believe it was their sacred duty to carry civilization west. A New York newspaper told them … "Our manifest destiny is to overspread and to possess the whole of the continent which Providence has given us for the development of the great experiment of liberty and federated self-government".

That was all they needed!

The major trails began at Independence, Missouri, jumping off place for the Santa Fe Trail into the Southwest or the Oregon Trail that headed north toward the Columbia River. It was a boom town in the 1840's with pioneers arriving with huge families and all their belongings loaded into ox-drawn, canvas-covered wagons. They usually stopped there for a while, buying supplies, hiring a mountain man to guide them and organizing themselves into trains of at least 40 wagons.

They took cattle with them, so they had to wait in Independence until the grass on the prairie was abundant enough to feed the stock. And since they all believed in the code of "rugged individualism", it wasn't easy for them to organize themselves into congenial groups.

Once under way on the Oregon Trail, they found the Kansas and Nebraska countryside beautiful if ominously quiet and desolate. The boredom was often broken by wild rainstorms that washed out their camps and flooded the streams they had to cross.

The wagons travelled four or more abreast so they could be organized into protective squares if Indians attacked. The men walked with the oxen to keep them moving, the boys kept the cattle from straying and the women sat at the front of the wagon, usually knitting.

The going got rougher when they reached Chimney Rock in Western Nebraska and their wagon wheels began to sink into the sandy soil. They were usually out of firewood by then, and as there were no trees to cut, they cooked over buffalo chip fires. Fort Laramie, in Wyoming, offered them a chance to load fresh supplies, to repair their wagons and to steel themselves for the hard part of the trip, the Rockies.

The route across Wyoming toward Idaho was littered with cast-off furniture, abandoned to make the wagons less burdensome for the starving oxen. It was uphill all the way until they reached a pass that took them through the mountains and over the top to find even more hostile, barren country ahead.

If they were lucky enough to make it before winter, they settled down in Oregon and California. And they never looked back. Yet, oddly, even native Californians today refer to everything on the other side of the Mississippi as "back East".

The Oregon Trail was laid out by the Lewis and Clark expedition; the Santa Fe Trail was the route of mule trains and caravans of ox carts that carried American trade from Independence down into New Mexico. It stretched almost 800 miles across the desert and through Apache country, so it wasn't as popular with the early emigrants until gold fever hit them in 1849 and people started heading west for different reasons.

A third major route to the West began in Palmyra, New York, a small town near the Erie Canal. A man named Joseph Smith was plowing his field there one day when an angel, who said his name was Moroni, introduced him to God and His Son.

Smith wrote a book about it, which he called "The Book of Mormon", and started a whole new religion. Some people in Palmyra didn't like the idea and they ran Smith and his followers out of town. They had the same experience in Ohio and then in Missouri, but even as they kept moving, Smith's following was growing. They finally settled along the Mississippi in an Illinois town they called Nauvoo. Before long, it was the biggest city in the entire state, with 15,000 residents, and the Mormons thought they were safe at last. But they weren't; Nauvoo was surrounded by "Gentiles", as Smith called non-Mormons, who weren't too neighborly or tolerant of these people who were said to practice polygamy. When Smith ordered a newspaper destroyed because it was critical of him, the Gentiles made their move. They lynched Joseph Smith.

Brigham Young became their leader, and he took on the mission of leading his people to a new land where there were no Gentiles. They sold their houses in Nauvoo and built wagons to make a long trip to the Great Salt Lake, which had been discovered some years before by Western explorers.

A few had oxen to pull their wagons, but most loaded their belongings into hand carts and started the long walk west. By the fall of 1847, some 2,000 of them had reached the "Promised Land", but what they found there was a dry, sun-baked plain. They put themselves completely under the control of their church, and together made the valley bloom. Meanwhile, thousands of converts arrived from the East and from Europe, and a string of settlements sprang up. There were enough of them before long for Brigham Young to announce that they had established an independent nation. He called it "Deseret". The U.S. Government called it the Territory of Utah, but it took 50 years for them to make the idea stick.

Even the Civil War didn't slow down the rush to the West. In the year General Sherman marched through Georgia, some 75,000 people marched in wagon trains along the Oregon Trail. And after the war ended in 1865, freed slaves and war veterans poured across the Mississippi looking for adventure and opportunity. What they found was what they themselves created; the Wild West.

Most of the big cattle spreads were in Texas and Colorado, but the Texas ranchers drove their longhorns as far north as the Dakota Territory to fatten them up over the winter before shipping them to the slaughterhouses in Chicago. The cowboys who drove them a thousand miles north were a lusty lot who spent 16 hours a day in the saddle, choking on dust, watching out for marauding Indians, heading off stampedes and fighting rustlers and armed farmers who didn't like to see all those cows trampling their crops.

A trail drive averaged about 2,500 head of cattle which were driven an average of 1,500 miles. A trail boss, in charge of about a dozen cowboys and a cook, was completely responsible for the operation, and shared the profits once the cattle were sold. His cowhands were paid about $30 a month and board.

Naturally, all that work made them thirsty. The cowtowns along their routes obliged them with plenty to drink as well as friendly games of chance to help boost their income, and companionship to boost their morale. It was a tough life, often a short one, but to be a cowboy in the Wild West is still an American boy's fondest dream.

Cowboys, gunslingers and U.S. Marshals were only part of the population who tamed the Wild West, however. In 1862, President Lincoln signed a law that entitled any American citizen (or anyone who intended to become one) to 160 acres of land for nothing more than a small filing fee and a promise to live there and farm it for at least 5 years. Civil War veterans went by the thousands into Kansas and Nebraska, the Dakotas and Montana to take the Government up on its offer. Europeans were lured by the promise of a free farm, too, and in less than a generation the country's population doubled. The cowboys called the Homesteaders "Sod-busters". The law required them to be farmers, but the farms got in the way of the cattle drives. The Indians didn't like their fenced-in acres either, but they were clearly there to stay.

The cowboys and Indians had another enemy, too. Sheep herders. After the Spanish brought sheep to California, the Indians themselves helped spread herds into Colorado and Texas. By the time the "Sod-busters" began arriving, the "Woolies" had half a million head of sheep on the range and were at war with the cattle ranchers. One range war in Arizona lasted more than 5 years, and before it ended more than 30 men died. Up in Wyoming one night, masked men attacked four sheep camps, tied up the shepherds and clubbed 8,000 sheep to death.

In yet another scheme to encourage settlement of the West, the Government gave millions of acres of land to the railroads that were being built through the territory. The railroad companies mounted an advertising blitz telling Easterners, "You Need A Farm!" and thousands agreed. They carried their campaign into Europe, and Germans, Dutch, Swedes, Norwegians and Danes responded enthusiastically. In Minnesota and the Dakotas, the Scandinavian languages became more common than English.

So many people flowed into the West that the Government decided it was time to relocate the "Indian Territory". They forced the Creeks and Seminoles to sell some of their land and they called it "Oklahoma". On April 22, 1889, it was declared open under the Homestead Act, and before noon on that day almost 2 million acres had been claimed. Before the sun set, the cities of Guthrie and Oklahoma City had been established. Four years later, the Government bought out the Cherokee territory and 100,000 people moved in on the first day it was declared open.

Meanwhile, people were starving in Ireland; the political situation in Germany was driving people away, and in less than 30 years, beginning in 1831, 3,500,000 people from those two countries decided to become Americans. At the same time, another 1,500,000 migrated from other countries.

Between 1855 and 1890, more than 7 million arrived from Europe through New York alone! They kept coming for more than 60 years after that, and between 1890 and 1954, when the immigration laws were changed, 20 million people from just about every country in the world came to put their mark on America.

By 1872, it was apparent that expansion was dramatically changing the shape of the land. The Mountain men wouldn't have recognized their lonely territory, and the old frontiers in Ohio and Tennessee were completely tamed. To preserve some of the natural beauty of the land, the Government set aside a tract of more than 3,470 square miles (an area bigger than the Commonwealth of Puerto Rico), in Wyoming, Montana and Idaho, and called it Yellowstone National Park. It's the oldest and still the biggest of the country's 37 National Parks. Yellowstone hasn't changed much since hunters, trappers and Indians roamed there more than 200 years ago. It's wild country with moose, elk and more, including a huge population of bears. The territory is laced with geysers and natural hot springs, some with temperatures as high as 200°F. The best known, Old Faithful, sends a jet of water and steam 200 feet into the air every 65 minutes, as regular as clockwork. It's as much a symbol of America to many people as the Statue of Liberty.

Yellowstone straddles the Continental Divide, a range of high mountains that separates East from West. Rivers from the east of it flow toward the Atlantic; from the west, water flows towards the Pacific. Further north in Montana, and spilling across the Canadian border, the Continental Divide is at its spectacular best in Glacier National Park. It's home to bighorn sheep and grizzly bears and snow that never melts. It was named for the glaciers that carved its breathtaking valleys, but there are still glaciers there, and it's as much like Alaska as any other spot in the lower 48 States.

Daniel Boone would still recognize the country's most-visited National Park, the Great Smoky Mountains in North Carolina and Tennessee. He'd know the restored log buildings and split rail fences, he'd probably stop for a chat with the local blacksmith or pick up some corn meal at the gristmill. But he'd be a little surprised to find nature trails for cars. Actually, though, if he thought about it, he'd smile to think that the majority of the 8 million people who tour the Park every year never get out of their cars and that leaves the mountaintops and winding trails quiet and peaceful. It makes it possible to explore in the same way he did and possibly not run into anyone else doing the same thing.

Americans are very attached to their cars and rarely go anywhere without them. The result is that many see America as superhighways carefully designed to carry traffic around the small towns and big cities, with interchanges full of ugly gas stations, tacky motels and fast food stands. Others in search of America fly over it in big jets and hope there are no clouds over the Grand Canyon to ruin the view.

It's a part of America that exists, there's no denying it. But there's another America out there. And it's worth exploring.

Way out West in the wilds of New Mexico, there's a roadside oasis that's a combination gas station, general store, restaurant, meat market and dance hall. On Friday nights, folks drop in for a little companionship, a little gossip, a little something to eat and a few beers. Some of them travel as far as 100 miles for the pleasure, because people are few and far between out there. The population is 0.3 persons per square mile, in fact.

The Friday night get-togethers are repeated in dozens of places along the old cattle driving routes. They were generally spaced about a day's drive apart and usually boasted a well. Today they pump gas instead of water and their customers arrive in pickup trucks rather than on horseback. But they bring the spirit of the West along with them. It's here that they buy all their gas and most of their food. And when they feel like a night on the town, they drop around for a T-bone steak and salad. They buy toys for their kids and batteries for their trucks. They go to make phone calls, because many never bothered to install phones at home. And if the Friday night party lasts too long, they stay the night in the attached motel.

In one of them on a Friday night not too long ago a woodcutter, who said he worked from six in the morning until sundown, seven days a week, summed up what it's all about: "When you're working that hard, that late, that long, you sure do appreciate a place like this to come and have a beer and relax", he said. And why does he work "that late, that long?" "Sometimes I hate to come in", he added, "it gets so pretty out there it hurts your eyes".

Up among the cornfields in the Midwest, the rhythm of life is a little different. People live in small towns with populations of five or six hundred on tree-shaded streets that criss-cross a main road where the stores are located. In most of them, the supper hour is announced at six in the evening with a blast from the siren on top of the firehouse. An hour later, the younger children drift downtown for an ice cream cone. They hang around for a while, but eventually they're replaced by teenagers out for a Coke and some companionship. They arrive on motorbikes or in souped-up cars with the rear-ends high in the air and the radios turned up even higher. When they get tired of the pinball games at the local drive-in, they drive up and down the quiet streets impressing the girls on the sidewalk by "peeling rubber" as they take off from a traffic light. It doesn't take them long to get bored with all that fun, and they soon settle down for a serious discussion about the high school football team; about girls, if they're boys, or about boys, if they're girls. By 11, the town has shut down for the night, and the only sounds are from crickets or a truck just passing through.

While their kids are enjoying themselves downtown, their parents are probably sitting out on the front porch, talking softly with a neighbor, listening to the sounds of the night, or complaining about all the racket those youngsters are making with their cars. Some nights they go downtown themselves. Down to the Elks or the Moose or the American Legion clubhouse. In many small towns in the middle of America, the fraternal organizations are at the center of the social life. They promote Americanism, the old values, neighborliness. And they provide a place to have a friendly drink and good conversation. They might sponsor bingo games for the ladies, poker parties for their husbands and buffet dinners for the whole family. On Saturday night, they pull out all the stops and turn the lodge hall into a dance hall where folks can take a turn to the music of Glenn Miller or Lawrence Welk, or swing and sway with Sammy Kaye.

Down in Georgia and Alabama and other parts of the Old South, community life is more often centered around the churches. One of the lures of the fraternal orders has always been to provide a place where an upstanding businessman could have a relaxing stinger or a grasshopper without running the risk of losing customers who might see him leaving the local saloon. In many parts of the South "Temperance" is too important a virtue for businessmen or politicians to unwind anywhere but behind the closed doors of their own homes.

The Southern churches, usually Methodist or Baptist, claim to give them all the unwinding they need, with singing and praying and inspiring preaching. Everybody goes to Sunday school, and the church supper is an event no one ever misses. To get ready for one, the ladies prepare casseroles, cakes, puddings, fried chicken, hams and biscuits. When it all comes together, it's one of life's great pleasures. These Southern Protestants deny themselves one of the things other Americans consider a pleasure: dancing. Not long ago a preacher in Knoxville, Tennessee, explained it to his parish by telling them: "Any man who says he can dance and keep his thoughts pure is less than a man or he is a liar!" The congregation, as they often do, answered him with a chorus of "Amens".

Sometimes Americans seek their pleasure by travelling abroad. But in their hearts, they know home's best. A woman in Dubuque, Iowa, explained how she felt: "It was wonderful to get back to the Old World charm of Dubuque. You know, the hills here are very reminiscent of Switzerland. And, oh, our river! Now, I've never seen anything, neither the Danube nor the Seine, that's as beautiful as the Mississippi".

A lot of them travel around the United States sharing the pleasures of other regions. They travel in mobile homes, in pickup trucks with little house-like affairs set precariously in the back and up over the roof, and they travel in cars. For those in cars who aren't packing their own sleeping quarters, there are more then 55,000

motels waiting to serve them, and a decade ago, Holiday Inns reported that they were adding a new motel to the landscape every 72 hours!

In quieter times when there were no Interstate Highways and cars didn't go over 30, people stayed overnight as paying guests in private houses that called themselves "tourist homes".

A lot of them still exist in small towns all across the country, but since the network of concrete spaghetti they call "super" highways take tourists over and around the small towns, tourist homes are being starved out even though they charge about half as much as the fancy motels. A typical tourist home might be a big old Victorian house on a town's main street; the yard studded with bright orange daylillies, the lawn shaded by tall old trees. The proprietors are often a retired couple living otherwise on a Social Security pension, and you can find them relaxing on the wide porch in front of the house. The rooms set aside for the "paying guests" are scrupulously clean and simply furnished. The twin beds may have been bought as surplus from a local hospital, and are probably the most comfortable anyone ever slept in. And sometimes for a pittance of an extra charge, a tourist can begin the new day with a home-cooked breakfast. It's a slice of life left over from the 1930's, and though many people claim to long for those times when life was slower and people seemed friendlier, they blithely pass it by. Leaving it to die.

The old ways are alive and well in many parts of the country, though. In New England clambakes, in Louisiana crawfish festivals, Oklahoma rodeos and Iowa tractor-pulling contests. Traditions like the Memorial Day parade, the Fourth of July picnic, Little League baseball and Sunday afternoon softball games bind us all to each other as well as to the past. High school football, band concerts and senior proms give us a sense of community. The beauty and abundance of the land itself gives us a sense of pride.

Express passenger trains don't roar across the plains any more. Hillbillies have been transplanted to "Dee-troit City" from the mountains of West Virginia. And a lot of the cotton fields down South are producing soybeans these days. But they still ride to hounds on the Eastern Shore in Maryland. They still play sweet Dixieland music in New Orleans. They still make Bourbon from good Kentucky corn and produce more beer than any other nation on earth.

Dodge City, Kansas, "the wickedest little city in the world" in Bat Masterson's day, is a little bit bigger and a whole lot less wicked these days. It's a tidy, prosperous city, home to 17,000 people who make farm machinery and drum heads and fatten cattle on their way to market. They also run a thriving business catering to tourists who are dying to see the cemetery up on Boot Hill. The women who live there these days are more likely to be dressed in blue jeans than calico. And none of the men carries a six-gun any more.

Blue jeans, like jazz and corn on the cob, are America's gift to the world. But more important is America's spirit and enthusiasm, a thing they call "The American Dream".

From the first day the first settler arrived from Europe, Americans have been excited about the idea that anything is possible. You can start from nothing and be somebody. You can control your own destiny, realize your wildest dream; or even be free not to be a superachiever if that's what your dream is all about.

Back in 1959, Nikita Khruschev toured the United States from New York to Coon Rapids, Iowa to Hollywood, California. When he arrived in movieland he was given the red carpet treatment in a tour of the studios of 20th Century Fox guided by no less a person than Spiros Skouras, the president of the company.

That evening at dinner, Skouras, one of the great movie czars of all time, explained to the Russian Premier that he had originally arrived in the United States as a penniless immigrant from Greece. "Only in America", he said, "could a young man with such humble beginnings make it straight to the top".

"I understand that very well", answered Khruschev. "My father was a coal miner in Soviet Georgia".

Putdowns notwithstanding, the American Dream works. At the last count, more than half a million Americans, a quarter of one percent of the population, reported a net worth of over a million dollars. Most of them live in New York and California, and Texas ranks tenth in millionaire population after Indiana, Idaho and Minnesota. Take that, Neiman-Marcus!

And every year, thousands of immigrants still renounce foreign princes and potentates in an oath that makes them American citizens. The busiest naturalization center in the country is, appropriately, in Brooklyn, New York. Some 30,000 take the oath there every year in a courtroom decorated with original murals from the now-closed immigration center on Ellis Island in New York harbor.

The murals show laborers working with picks and shovels, but the new citizens are more likely to be computer programmers than mine workers. Immigrants these days are more middle class, better educated and younger than the Irish, Italian and Middle European people who crowded through New York a generation ago.

They come from more diverse places, too. Not long ago, on a day 329 potential citizens arrived in that Brooklyn courtroom, the majority, 49 of them, came from Jamaica. The rest were from 55 different countries, including one Russian, and a Greek who had written a song that had been a hit in America ten years before.

The judge who administered the oath is himself the son of an Italian immigrant and has been naturalizing foreign-born citizens for two decades. The process takes about three hours, including a literacy test, which these days about 95 per cent of the applicants pass easily. Some of them change their names along with their nationality, like Harry Gerolymatos, who decided to Americanize himself to Harris Gerolymatos.

And why do they go to the trouble? A Pakistani immigrant explained: "I decided it is better to be a citizen of the country, the people of which reached the moon. Even if I do not reach the moon, I want to be among the people who reached the moon".

Once having taken the oath, nothing at all distinguishes them from all the other American citizens. They move on to places like Moscow, Pa, Cairo, Ga, Bagdad, Arizona or Paradise, Michigan.

Some might go to Canton, Ill., which was named for Canton, China, which the original settlers were sure would be reached if you dug a deep enough hole. Or out to West Texas where a cowboy once said, "You can lie on your belly and see for miles. Of course, there ain't nothing to see, but if there was, you could see it".

They could send their children to a one-room schoolhouse in Nebraska. They could get a job in a monster shopping mall just about anywhere. They can do just about anything they want. Anything, that is, except run for President. But as native-born Americans, their children can become President, possibly even their girl-children.

And that, above all, is what the American Dream is all about.

Light filters through the trees, patterning the golden carpet of leaves at Woodstock, in Vermont *left,* which has been restored to preserve its elegant 18th and 19th century buildings.

The beauty of fall in the 'Green Mountain State' – Vermont – which is covered almost entirely by an extension of the Appalachian Mountain system, is shown in all its subtlety and variety of color in the pictures *above, right* and *below.*

Although the lovely state of Vermont is primarily rural there are many attractive and distinctive towns and villages harmoniously blended into its landscape. Vermont has something to offer all the year round. In the summer there are long, sunny days and the winter brings its own wonderland.

Skiing is pictured *above* at Stowe, and *left* the last moments of daylight color the sky above Mount Ethan Allen.

Beautifully preserved houses at Brandon are shown *above right* and *right,* and *below* is the church at Pittsford.

Equally well preserved is the Marshfield General Store *below right* and Shelburne railroad station *below far right.*

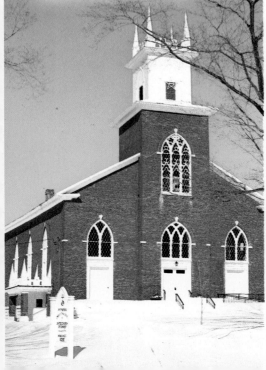

New Hampshire is another of the lovely states that go to make up that renowned part of America known as New England. Forest trails, rivers and lakes, as well as mountains, are very much a feature of New Hampshire. The state was the only one of the original thirteen that remained unscarred during the War of Independence.

Sited in the densely forested White Mountains *bottom left and above,* the state's snow-peaked pride, is Bethlehem *bottom,* pictured as fall's russet tones tint the landscape. Bethlehem's catholic church is shown *top,* and a farm near West Thornton *top left,* while *center left* can be seen the weatherboard buildings at Tufton Corner.

One of New Hampshire's sixty carefully preserved covered or 'kissing' bridges is shown at Blair on the Beebe River *right,* and the boulder-strewn Saco River *above right.*

The state of Maine, situated in the far northeast of the United States, is renowned for its spectacular, rugged coastline. Lighthouses, such as Portland Lighthouse *right,* which dates back to 1791, and the construction of which was ordered by George Washington, are an essential feature of the rocky and often dangerous coastline.

Sailing boats and pleasure cruisers provide a welcome means of relaxation, and a safe anchorage is provided by the many harbors, such as Northeast Harbor, Acadia National Park *above* and Booth Bay *left.* There are still those who earn their living on the sea, including the lobster fishermen *below.*

The beauty of Maine's coastline is epitomised *overleaf* by the sun setting behind Bass Harbor Headlight, set in the cliffs of the Acadia National Park.

24

Camden River's waterfalls run below the main street in Camden *above* and cascade into the harbor, from where graceful schooners sail the Maine coast.

Pictured *top right* are the Hamilton Laboratory Farm Buildings in Acadia National Park.

The Sea Grill Restaurant, decorated with colorful window boxes *above,* is characteristic of Maine's smaller settlements lying in wooded settings *left.*

Although it is now several miles from the sea, Wiscasset *center right* was once a seafaring town and the principal port east of Boston. Like Bath *below right,* it was noted for its ship-building and has been carefully preserved in its picturesque setting.

Behind the brilliant colors of fall foliage stands the church at Bethel *below.*

A solitary house set among the trees is reflected *overleaf* in the Androscoggin River at Rumford, in Maine.

Boothbay Harbor, Maine *above,* is at the unspoilt center of a busy resort area in Acadia National Park.

A home in Blue Hill Village *far left* nestles among the russet-colored fall foliage.

The stone church *left,* at York, was built in 1808 and the church *below* is at Gorham.

Fallen leaves add a touch of color to the still waters of a lake in Maine *above right.*

Fort Edgecomb *center right,* in Acadia National Park, is a remnant of the 1812 war and now a much-visited historic site.

Dramatic cliffs *below right* rise from the waters of the Atlantic ocean at Cape Elizabeth.

Boston's magnificent State House *above,* with its gilded dome, was designed by Charles Bulfinch in 1795.

Serving as one of the principal exhibits in the Boston Tea Party Museum is the authentic replica of the Brig Beaver II *right,* one of three ships involved in the notorious Boston Tea Party.

The U.S.S. Frigate "Constitution" *left,* known as "Old Ironsides", was restored and rebuilt in 1833 and is another important tourist attraction, and the bas-relief *below* adorns one of the monuments on Boston Common.

Boston by night is seen *overleaf* from across Charles River.

Pictured *left* is the First Church of Christ
Scientist, which nestles, almost incongruously,
amid the high-rise buildings *above*.
The beautiful interior of the Paul Revere
House contains many original furnishings.
Situated at North Square, the house was
purchased by the master silversmith in 1770
and it is now the oldest surviving wooden
structure in Boston. *Below* is shown one of the
delightful bedrooms.
Charles River is featured *top right* deep in the
grip of winter, deserted except for flocks of
birds.

In the immediate foreground of the aerial view
below is part of the Public Garden and, next to
it, Boston Common. These two green and
pleasant parks are set in the heart of the city,
with historic Beacon Hill to the north. At the
far end of the Common can be seen the
distinctive dome of the New State House.
Modern Boston, with its towering blocks, so
typical of most American cities, is pictured
center right and right.
Deerfield, Massachusetts *overleaf* is a village
that has been designated a National Historic
District.

Duxbury *top left,* once a quiet farming community, became a prosperous shipping center in the 19th century. In addition to a number of architecturally noteworthy buildings, Duxbury also boasts one of the finest beaches in New England.

Weatherboarded houses blend perfectly into the rolling pastures, woodlands and lakes that are such a feature of the area around Sturbridge *above.*

Deerfield, Massachusetts, a National Historic District village, is famed for the restoration of its public buildings. Many of them are now over 150 years old for, despite the numerous Indian attacks which, from 1672–1704 virtually destroyed the village, it has now been delightfully recreated. *Center left* is the Rev. Jonathan Ashley House, *below left* is the Sheldon-Hawks House, and *above right* the Dwight-Barnard House Museum.

Harvard University *right* was founded in 1636 and is America's oldest institution of higher learning. It was named after John Harvard, a Puritan Minister, who bequeathed his library and half his estate to the university, an act of generosity commemorated by a statue on the campus *below.*

Small bays, inlets, beaches and the rolling countryside of Massachusetts; all are transformed by winter's blanket of snow, made sparkling by sunshine and blue skies at Duxbury *above, center left and below left,* Deerfield *right and top left* and on the campus of Harvard University *below.*

Historic Provincetown *above,* with its McMillan Wharf, is the point where the Pilgrims first made landfall before continuing to Plymouth in the Mayflower *left.*

Cape Cod was first discovered in 1602 by the English navigator Bartholomew Gosnold, who named it after the large shoals of cod he found there. Today its rolling sand dunes *right* and great natural beauty such as Buzzard Bay *above right* are complemented by many picturesque buildings, like Chatham Lighthouse *below,* which all combine to make the area a popular tourist resort.

46

Hartford *above,* Connecticut's state capital and largest city, is the home of many major insurance and other companies, housed in towering buildings which, at night, cast their glittering reflections on the waters of the Connecticut River.

The gold-domed Capitol Building *left and right* which was once described as a "Gothic Taj Mahal", sits dramatically on the highest point of Bushnell Park.

Below is Nook Farm, Mark Twain's house in Hartford.

New Haven, Connecticut's third largest city, is famous above all for Yale University, featured on *these pages and previous page.*

Founded in 1701, Yale was named after Elihu Yale who, in 1718, made a substantial donation to what was then a college. As an institution of higher learning it acquired university status in 1887 and in 1969 these beautiful old doors opened to admit women students.

Stone-mullioned and leaded windows and ivy-clad walls help to lend an air of history to Yale's lovely old buildings and colleges as they bask in the New England sunshine.

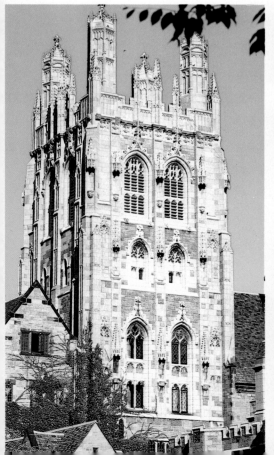

Connecticut represents a special blending of modern urban life with a deep sense of its history and environment. Crystal clear rivers and lakes *left;* quiet village greens surrounded by gracious homes; old stone houses such as the Henry Whitfield State Historical Museum at Guildford *right,* believed to be the oldest stone house in New England; golden beaches and peaceful harbors like Mystic Seaport *above* and the charm of the white, steepled Congregational church dominating Litchfield Green *above right,* are all typical of the beauty of this lovely part of New England.

The well-preserved covered wagon *below* survives as a relic of days long past.

Rhode Island is the smallest state in the U.S.A., but within its boundaries it contains considerable variety.

Providence, the state capital, is an important deep water port *center left* and commercial center. Pictured *top left* is the County Court House, constructed in 1933, while *above* is a church in old Providence.

Bottom left may be seen a view of downtown Providence, and *below* is a farm, typical of many in the area.

The imposing State House, featuring the second largest unsupported marble dome in the world, is pictured *right,* and *above* pumpkins are arranged to ripen on the lawn of a gracious country house.

The border between Canada and New York State is formed by the Niagara River, which provides the water for the most popular of U.S. tourist attractions, Niagara Falls, half of which, known as Horseshoe Falls *below,* are actually in Canada. Most often seen in the summer months, the falls take on a totally different, though no less awe-inspiring, appearance *these pages and overleaf* when almost brought to a standstill by the icy grip of winter.

59

Of all the world's statues none can be more famous or instantly recognizable than the Statue of Liberty *left*. It was originally created in France by Frédéric-Auguste Bartholdi and represents Liberty, freed from her chains and holding aloft, in her right hand, a torch. Cradled in her left arm is a tablet representing the Declaration of Independence.

The streets of New York are constantly alive with traffic and incident *this page,* some everyday, some dramatic.

Overleaf and on the following two pages is shown the vast complexity of steel, concrete and glass that goes to make up the familiar face of Manhattan.

The land on which the Rockefeller Center is built belongs to Columbia University, to which institution it was left by Dr. David Hosack. At the back of the plaza stands Paul Manship's huge, golden statue of Prometheus *right*.

For many years the Empire State Building *above* was the world's tallest skyscraper and, despite being exceeded in height by other buildings, it still remains the symbol of skyscrapers everywhere.

The magnificent bronze statue *below,* on Fifth Avenue, represents Atlas, supporting on his shoulders a symbolic earth.

Central Park, that haven of trees and grass, the 'lung' of Manhattan, is used and enjoyed by New Yorkers and visitors *top, center and bottom left* for a variety of purposes.

Overleaf is shown the Manhattan skyline from New Jersey, and on the following pages the center of Manhattan in the grip of winter.

Except for its 48 mile boundary with New York State, New Jersey is washed on all sides by water. Its beaches *left* attract countless vacationers each year. Atlantic City *below*, has recently introduced casinos to the Boardwalk and is rapidly regaining its popularity as one of the country's leading resorts. Behind the beaches the rolling landscape reveals a checkerboard of lush pastureland *above* – over 65 percent of the land area being farms and forests. Included in New Jersey's famous historic sites is the Ford Mansion, Morristown *above right,* where George Washington made his headquarters during the winter of 1779–80. Barnegat Light *right and overleaf,* perched on the tip of Long Beach Island, looks out over the Atlantic Ocean.

74

Gettysburg, Pennsylvania *above*, seen from the National Tower *above left*, is famous as the site of the momentous battle, in July 1863, which marked the turning point in the Civil War. Commemorating the event is the memorial *below*, in the National Military Park, which also includes the National Cemetery *right* and *below left*.

Pittsburgh, at the confluence of the Allegheny and Monongahela Rivers, is pictured by night *overleaf*.

78

Delaware, the second smallest state of the Union, provides a wealth of interest for visitors with its small, picturesque towns, historic sites and tranquil countryside *below.* Built by Swedes in 1638, after the founding of Wilmington, the Old Swedes Church *right* is believed to be the oldest Protestant church still in use in America, while at New Castle *left* can be seen the early 18th century Immanuel Episcopal church.

Reedy Point Bridge *above* is one of a series of bridges, causeways and tunnels which span the entrance to Chesapeake Bay.

Maryland, named for the wife of King Charles I by Lord Baltimore in 1632, displays a great diversity of landscape in spite of its relatively small size. At the foot of the forested Appalachians nestle the isolated farms *left* and *bottom right;* at Emmitsburg is located Mount St. Mary's College, with its lovely chapel *top right* and Seminary *center right,* and the Memorial *above and below,* which commemorates Mother Seton, the first native-born American to be canonized.

85

Among the many fine monuments to be found in Washington D.C., the nation's gracious capital, are the White House *above;* the slender white marble column of the Washington Memorial *below,* which dominates the skyline beyond Arlington Cemetery *left;* the Hellenistic Supreme Court Building *right;* the impressive Jefferson Memorial *overleaf* and the magnificent Capitol *previous page.*

Washington, one of the world's most beautiful capitals, is also a noted cultural and educational center and its museums and art galleries, shrines and monumental buildings attract countless visitors from all parts of the globe. *Above* is shown the polygonal East Building of the National Gallery of Art; *right* the Smithsonian Institution's Natural History Building; *below left* the spectacular free-moving globe in Explorers Hall: *below* the shimmering sphere in the Sculpture Garden of the Hirshhorn Museum; *above left* the Washington Monument and *overleaf* the majestic Lincoln Memorial.

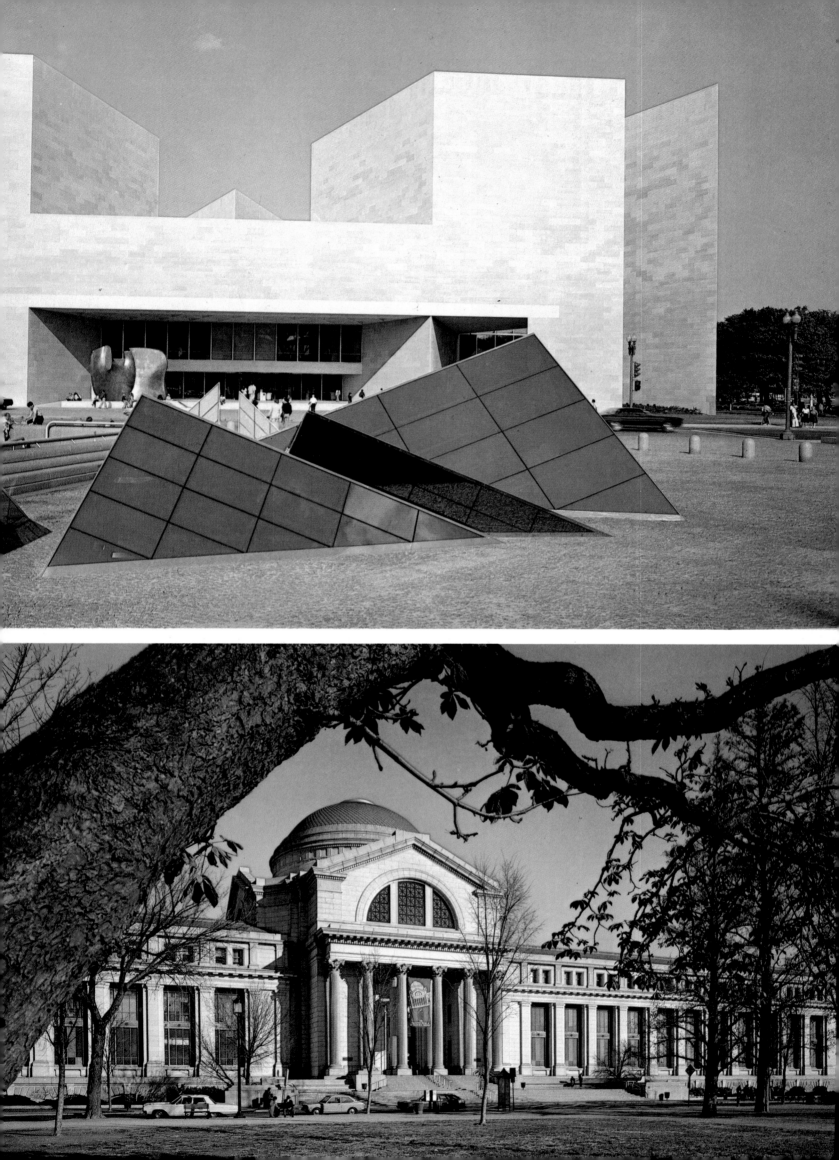

Kentucky, renowned for its fine thoroughbred horses, which grow sleek on the rich pasture of the Bluegrass *above,* has preserved its historic heritage whilst developing its natural resources to become a flourishing industrial state. Among its many attractions are the Abraham Lincoln Birthplace National Historic Site *left;* the beautiful State Capitol at Frankfort *above left;* St. Joseph's Cathedral at Bardstown *below,* and a familiar riverboat *right,* pictured as it plies the waters of the Ohio River at Louisville.

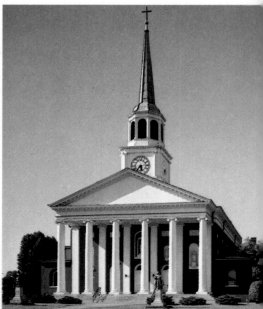

Nashville, Tennessee's state capital, is a city of contrasts, evidenced by the State Capitol *top and bottom left*, an outstanding example of Ionic Greek architecture; the Parthenon *center left*, a full-sized replica of the original at Athens and sited in Centennial Park; the Country Music Hall of Fame and Museum *below*, and the lovely Belle Meade Mansion *right*, the first of the country's thoroughbred stud farms.

Memphis *above*, one of the world's largest spot cotton markets, is a fine modern city particularly noted for its educational and medical facilities.

Winston-Salem, in North Carolina, still retains the traditions and architecture of its pioneer settlers, typified by the Apothecary *above right* and the Elm House Tavern *center right*, with its traditionally furnished kitchen *below*.

Charleston, the official state port of South Carolina, is one of the country's oldest and most historic cities and its notable buildings include the Dock Street Theater and lofty steepled St. Philip's Church *left* and St. Michael's Episcopal Church *above*, modelled on St. Martin's-in-the-Field, London; while lovely old plantation houses such as Drayton Hall *bottom right* are a particular feature of the South Carolina landscape.

Constructed in 1809 for one of Charleston's first merchants, the Nathaniel Russell House is an outstanding example of Adam-style architecture. Its magnificent oval drawing-rooms *center left* and *below right*, and the dining-room *above right*, are elegantly decorated with furnishings of the period.

America's oldest landscaped gardens, at Middleton Place, are exquisitely laid out, with rolling terraces, classically formal gardens, wooded walks, and tranquil butterfly lakes seen *previous page*, overhung by heavy summer foliage. Built in 1755, the house *top left*, although originally the guest wing, became the main residence when the chief part of the house was destroyed by fire during the Civil War. Within the grounds can also be seen the Rice Mill *bottom left*, which now displays exhibits describing the cultivation of rice.

Cotton plants *above*, in sleepy cotton fields, are reminiscent of the great plantation days before the Civil War when the fields would be filled with slaves who lived in cottages on the vast estates, like Boone Hall Plantation, where nine original slave houses, lining the 'Avenue of Oaks' *below*, have been preserved.

Within the Shenandoah Valley of West Virginia, a magnificent national park of outstanding beauty, with its sparkling streams, forested trails and mountain peaks, is historic Harper's Ferry, sited at the confluence of the swirling Shenandoah River *right*, and the peaceful Potomac *above left*. The old foot bridge *above*, and picturesque Shenandoah Farm *below left* can be seen in the beautiful landscape surrounding the town.

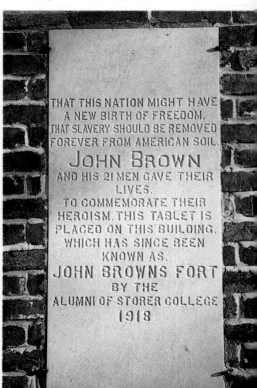

THAT THIS NATION MIGHT HAVE
A NEW BIRTH OF FREEDOM,
THAT SLAVERY SHOULD BE REMOVED
FOREVER FROM AMERICAN SOIL.
JOHN BROWN
AND HIS 21 MEN GAVE THEIR
LIVES.
TO COMMEMORATE THEIR
HEROISM. THIS TABLET IS
PLACED ON THIS BUILDING,
WHICH HAS SINCE BEEN
KNOWN AS,
JOHN BROWNS FORT
BY THE
ALUMNI OF STORER COLLEGE
1918

It was at Harper's Ferry, in 1859, that John Brown launched his anti-slavery raid against the County Militia and Citizen Volunteers in a bid to capture the U.S. Arsenal and Armory. The brave attempt proved vain, however, for Brown and a few of his followers were driven to the Fire-Engine House, now known as John Brown's Fort *above right*, where they remained until the following day. Brown was subsequently captured and tried, and sentenced to death by hanging. Commemorating the act of heroism is the memorial plaque *previous page*, placed in the wall of the fort by the Alumni of Storer College in 1918. The old houses lining the narrow streets of the town *bottom left*, have recently been restored to show their mid-19th century appearance and the Dry Goods Store *center left* and *right* is a particularly fine example. *Top left*, *above* and *below* are further lovely examples of the scenery along the Shenandoah River.

Colonial Williamsburg, carefully restored to capture the atmosphere and appearance of its 18th century existence, formed the capital of the colony of Virginia between 1699 and 1799. The aim of the preservation project, begun in 1926 and administered by the Colonial Williamsburg Foundation, was to recreate this colorful period of American history, and beautifully exemplifying the Foundation's aims are the picturesque houses and shops *these pages and overleaf left* and the delightful taverns, such as Chownings *top right*. The Governor's lovely Palace *overleaf right*, served as both home and office for several royal governors under the British Crown.

111

Among the most popular attractions of the historic Market Square area are the exciting musters of the colorfully costumed Colonial Williamsburg militia company *this page* which take place throughout the seasons.

The presentations include tactical demonstrations of muskets and cannons, drilling, and special salutes, to the accompaniment of fifes and drums.

A golden sunset casts a warm glow over the deserted snow-filled streets *right*.

Monticello *top left,* Thomas Jefferson's beautiful home, which is dominated by a shining white dome, is an outstanding example of classic American architecture. Its magnificently furnished rooms include many personal mementoes of the noted statesman. Richmond's majestic Capitol Building, seen *above* banked by winter's snow and *bottom left* as summer's foliage frames its elegant façade, was designed by Thomas Jefferson and modeled on the Maison Carree, an ancient Roman temple at Nimes.

The famous Washington Monument *below,* the celebrated equestrian statue of George Washington by Thomas Crawford, stands in Capitol Square, just beyond the main entrance to the Capitol Building.

Commemorating the one hundredth anniversary of the Siege of Yorktown is the 95-foot granite shaft of the Victory Monument *center left,* the cornerstone of which was laid by President Chester A. Arthur in 1881.

The distinctive red Nicolson's shop *below* is a further charming example of one of Colonial Williamsburg's carefully preserved clapboard buildings.

Reconstructions of forts built by the early pioneer settlers and huts which were once used by the Indians, are part of the fascinating exhibits at Jamestown Festival Park *above,* constructed in 1957 to mark the 350th anniversary of the momentous landing.

Berkeley *below,* believed to be the oldest three-story brick house in Virginia, was built in 1726 by Benjamin Harrison, while Westover *above right,* a fine example of Georgian architecture set in charming landscaped grounds, was built about 1730, by William Byrd II, the founder of Richmond.

Typical of many Virginia courthouses, with its octagonal cupola and arched windows, the T-shaped Courthouse of 1770 *right* stands in the center of Colonial Williamsburg's Market Square.

Arkansas, a beautiful vacation land featuring prairies, mountains and deep deltas, contains the country's only diamond mine. Little Rock, its lovely capital, nicknamed "City of Roses", was settled in 1814 on a rocky bluff overlooking the Arkansas River, and *overleaf* can be seen its superb white marble and granite State Capitol Building.

Natchez, Mississippi, still retains its colorful 'Old South' atmosphere, particularly in the gracious ante-bellum mansions such as those at Biloxi *below right*; the lovely Glen Auburn *right*; the classically-designed Melrose *below*, and Dr. Haller Nutt's Moorish-inspired mansion, Longwood *top left*, with its beautifully furnished interior *center left* and *bottom*.

Civil War cannons, placed in their original battery positions *below left*, together with the memorial in the background, and the statue, *top of page*, are on view in the Vicksburg National Military Park.

New Orleans *above*, the largest city in Louisiana, is one of the country's most colorful – its major attraction undoubtedly the fascinating French Quarter, or Vieux Carré, with narrow streets, lovingly-restored old buildings exquisitely adorned with lace iron-work balconies *top left*, popular venues such as Pat O'Brien's Patio *bottom left* and famous jazz clubs.

Jackson Square *right*, located in the heart of the Vieux Carré, and originally the Place d'Armes, was transformed, in 1856, from a dusty parade ground into a beautiful garden park, its focal point the bronze equestrian statue of Andrew Jackson, created by Clark Mills. Behind the statue can be seen the basilica of St. Louis Cathedral, completed in 1794 as part of the beneficence of Don Andres Almonester de Roxas.

From the streetcar *below* can be glimpsed the lovely old plantation houses on St. Charles Avenue *center left*, while 'Natchez' *overleaf*, a magnificent sternwheeler steamer, provides a memorable experience as it plies the muddy waters of the Mississippi.

122

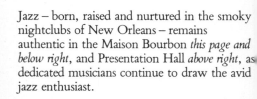

Jazz – born, raised and nurtured in the smoky nightclubs of New Orleans – remains authentic in the Maison Bourbon *this page and below right*, and Presentation Hall *above right*, as dedicated musicians continue to draw the avid jazz enthusiast.

The music that began as a functional accompaniment to weddings and funerals, dances and parades, was improvised by talented artists who produced the haunting 'blues' melodies that spread to St. Louis, Chicago and New York, and although in its later development it became more sophisticated, in essence it still belongs to New Orleans, this southern city which cradled so many of those who were to become numbered among the world's finest jazz musicians.

126

For the dedicated musicians who play in the nightclubs of the Vieux Carré *these pages*, jazz is more than just another number for an appreciative audience – it is a way of life – so clearly evident in the rapt concentration displayed by these talented players.

Located in the beautiful 100-acre woodland setting of the Audubon State Commemorative Area, Oakley House, St. Francisville, Louisiana *above*, was built in 1799 and is closely associated with the noted naturalist and artist, John James Audubon, who painted thirty two of his famous series 'Birds of America' during his stay at the house as tutor to the daughter of Mr. and Mrs. James Pirrie.

Baton Rouge, Louisiana's gracious capital, contains a wealth of attractions including the Gothic-inspired Old State Capitol *above left*, which was constructed in 1847 and served as the state capitol until 1932, and the stately Governor's Mansion *bottom left*.

Within the Mississippi Valley can be seen the beautiful mansions of Tezcuzo *below right*; Houmas House, Burnside *below*, and Oak Alley *above right*, where giant oaks, reputedly over 250 years old, frame the lovely façade.

Center left is pictured the simplistic St. Gabriel's Catholic Church.

Containing personal furnishings of Jefferson Davis and his family, the First White House of the Confederacy *below*, in Montgomery, Alabama's state capital, is sited opposite the majestic Capitol Building *bottom right*. Shown *above and left* is the interior of Oakleigh, one of Mobile's loveliest mansions, and *top right* is Gaineswood, Demopolis, an outstanding Greek Revival structure elegantly furnished *center right* with genuine period pieces.

The circular Peachtree Plaza Hotel *overleaf* is one of the most familiar landmarks on Atlanta's skyline. As night falls across Georgia's state capital *above*, floodlights enhance the splendor of the gold-domed Capitol Building *below*, while a perpetual flame burns before the memorial to Dr. Martin Luther King, Jr., *right*.
Part of the Fourth of July celebrations, a dazzling firework display *left*, explodes over the imposing Atlanta Stadium.

134

The bronze statue of the Phoenix *below* symbolizes the drive and spirit of dynamic Atlanta, with its sumptuous hotels such as the Hyatt Regency *above right*; magnificent complexes evidenced in the Omni International Megastructure *above*; outstanding sports facilities, seen in the Atlanta Stadium *left*, and excellent educational facilities exemplified by Atlanta University *below right*.

Underground Atlanta, part of which is shown *above,* is now one of the most popular areas for entertainment and shopping. For years this oldest section of the city had lain deserted, covered by a vast viaduct system, constructed to allow the growing volume of traffic to flow unimpeded across the city center until, in the late 1960's, its restoration resulted in this unique 'city within a city'. Atlanta is the home of the world-famous Coca-Cola, and the barrel *below* is an exhibit in the Coca-Cola Building and Museum. Exciting scenes from Atlanta's Fourth of July Parade are shown *left and right.*

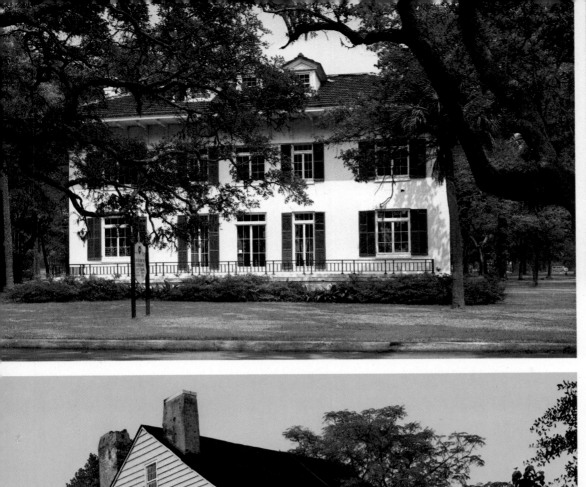

Preserved by the Atlanta Historical Society, the Tully Smith House *above*, originally constructed in 1840, is the center of a farm complex, complete with a log barn, slave cabin and double corn crib, which is an authentic example of a mid-19th century 'plantation plain' Georgia farmhouse. Set in the midst of Atlanta's Northside residential district is the Governor's Mansion *below*. Of Greek Revival style architecture, the mansion is handsomely furnished with 19th century American antiques of the Federal period. Jekyll Island and St. Simon's Island are two of the lovely semi-tropical islands along the Georgia coast which were claimed by Spain as the 'Golden Isles of Guale'. On Jekyll Island, once a favorite haunt of millionaires, can be seen the antebellum mansion *above right* and picturesque Good Year Cottage *top left*, while south of Fort Frederica, on St. Simon's Island, is Christ Church *below right*, which was founded by the Wesley brothers in 1736. The Olde Pink House, facing Reynolds Square *bottom left*, and the pretty clapboard house *center left*, are part of the rich heritage of Savannah, one of the most fascinating and historic cities of the South.

Each year millions of visitors from all over the world flock to Miami, Florida *these pages*, to the mainland and downtown Miami *center left*, but above all to Miami Beach, the island just across Biscayne Bay. Fifty years ago Miami Beach was a wilderness of mangrove swamps infested with snakes and mosquitoes. Today a quarter of all the hotels in Florida are situated here in a slender strip of architectural virtuosity set among glistening beaches and turquoise waters.

Spectacular 23 foot leaps are regularly made by the black and white killer whales Hugo and Lolita *overleaf*, in the Miami Seaquarium.

Every year an incredible total of over 20,000,000 lbs of fish, crabs, lobsters, shrimps and sea turtles are marketed from Key West alone, and the sparkling waters that wash the whole island chain of the Florida Keys are rich in the marine life that provides both a necessary livelihood and a popular, exciting and demanding sport.

Not far from Orlando, Circus World *on these pages* provides the opportunity to relive the thrill of a bygone era when the circus came to town ... to laugh at the comic antics of the colorful clowns and to witness spectacular acts in the finest tradition of family entertainment.

Awe-inspiring spacecraft dominate the Kennedy Space Center *overleaf.*

153

The Wild West still fires the imagination of small boys – and perhaps those not so small – all over the world. Not far from Ocala, Six Gun Territory *these pages* provides a vivid reconstruction of many of the colorful stories from America's past. Bank robberies, shoot-outs and quick justice are all re-enacted by characters in the appropriate dress and settings of days gone by.

Chicago, Illinois, the hub of the vast Middle West, is the country's second largest city, commanding a prime position along the southern shores of Lake Michigan. This vital and industrious city has a tradition of architectural inventiveness that is evident in the spectacular increase in its glossy buildings, and Chicago is proud of the fact that it was here that the first metal framed skyscraper was built – William Le Baron Jenney's Home Insurance Company Building – during 1884-85.

Among Chicago's gleaming towers which line the waterfront *above*, can be seen the terra-cotta encased Wrigley Building and the Gothic skyscraper of the Tribune Tower *top left*, while *overleaf* the aerial view provides a stunning panorama of the city and its skyline.

North Lake Shore Drive can be seen *right*, and *left* is Soldier Field, the remodelled war memorial which is now the home of the Chicago Bears football team.

By night Chicago's awe-inspiring skyline *top left* is a truly magnificent sight as city lights pierce the darkened sky and cast a glittering reflection along the waterfront on North Lake Shore Drive *above* and *center left*, and across Lake Michigan *right*.

Spectacularly illuminated, the Buckingham Memorial *bottom left* stands in Grant Park, while *below*, against a night sky can be seen the immense Sears Tower.

Chicago, offering a wealth of recreational facilities, is also a spirited, cultural, hard-working and financial center, evidenced in the varied aspects of community life illustrated on these pages. *Above* is shown the sculpture exhibit by Alexander Calder in the Sears Tower lobby; *top left* and *below right*, Lake Michigan; *center left* commuter traffic in the terminal of Union Station; *bottom left* the Trading Floor of the Mercantile Exchange on West Jackson Boulevard; *above right* the Bahai House of Worship; *below* the open air restaurant of the First National Bank, and *bottom* the Widebold Hall University Complex.

GOLD

162

163

Indiana, an important agricultural and industrial center, and popularly known as the 'Hoosier State', is also noted for its extensive system of state parks and forests as well as its outstanding educational facilities. One of the best known universities is that of Notre Dame in South Bend, which was founded in 1842; the lovely administration building of which can be seen *left*, its golden dome surmounted by a statue of the Virgin Mary. Named by the French, who settled the area in 1701, Detroit's name is derived from 'd'etroit' or 'straits', which refers to the 27-mile long Detroit River connecting the lakes of Erie and Clair. This fast-moving Michigan city is the largest automobile producing city in the world, aptly tagged 'Motor City' as shown *overleaf*. The densely-packed downtown area, where the New Renaissance Center *below* is sited, is shown *top right*, while the fountain *above* can be seen on Belle Isle, an island park in the Detroit River.

Miners Castle, part of the colorful rock formations of the Pictured Rocks National Lakeshore, is shown *bottom right*, and *center right* the Mackinac Straits Bridge, one of the world's longest suspension bridges.

Cincinnati, 'the Queen City of the West', is the third largest city in Ohio, connected to Covington, an industrial Kentucky town, by a series of bridges *above*, *right* and *below*. The beautiful Tyler Davidson bronze statue *left*, in Fountain Square, was sculpted by August von Kreling and dedicated to the people of Cincinnati in 1871.

Dayton, seen from the Plaza in the downtown area *above left*, was the home of the famous aviation pioneers Orville and Wilbur Wright.

Silos and dairies *top left* are a familiar feature of the Wisconsin landscape, for this sizable state plays a major role in the nation's production of dairy food. Popularly appealing to vacationers, the state's diversity is clearly shown in Algoma Harbor *center left*; Stonefield Village, Cassville *bottom left*; Door County, with the Cana Island Light *above*; pioneer homes at Mineral Point *right*, and Watertown Park *below*, in Milwaukee, the state's largest city.

170

Windmills *right* and prosperous farmhouses *above* nestle in the rolling pastureland of Iowa, one of the country's most intensely agricultural states, which produces some twenty percent of the nation's corn. Dubuque, the oldest city in Iowa, was named for Julien Dubuque, a French-Canadian, who established the first settlement here in 1788. The old town clock, relocated in the city's Downtown Mall, can be seen *left*, and *above left* the Delta Queen, in Government Locks. Amana, site of Pioneer House *below*, was the first village to be founded, in 1855, in the Amana Colonies, a group of seven closely-bound villages which is one of the state's major tourist attractions.

173

Over ninety percent of the vast, fertile plains of Kansas support livestock such as that *overleaf*, and crops, particularly wheat, that are so much a feature of this state. While agriculture plays a dominant role in the economy, manufacturing is also important, and as well as being major industrial cities, Wichita *top left* is a noted shipping center and Topeka, the capital, with its lovely state House *right*, an important rail center. Boot Hill *above* and Front Street *bottom left* are part of the historic complex of Dodge City *top* and *center left*, the notorious frontier town of the late 1800's.

Lying astride the great Mississippi River *center left*, the Twin Cities of Minneapolis and St. Paul are the educational, cultural and industrial centers of the northern Great Lakes region. Stately St. Paul *overleaf*, Minnesota's dignified capital, is an elegant, terraced city of lovely homes and majestic government buildings such as the State Capitol *right and below*. Designed by Cass Gilbert, the cornerstone was laid in 1898 and over 25 varieties of marble, granite, sandstone and limestone were used in the building's construction. A riverboat lies berthed in the icy Mississippi *above*, while from the snow-banked river can be seen downtown St. Paul across the Marina *top left*. Beautiful Minneapolis contains, within the city limits, 11 lakes and 156 lovely parks – one of the finest parks systems in the country – and its teeming industry and cultural pursuits are unsurpassed. The 57-story tower of the I.D.S. Center in downtown Minneapolis *bottom left*, is one of four buildings in the complex, which also contains the popular, glass-enclosed courtyard of Crystal Court.

Built of Carthage marble, the outstanding State Capitol of Jefferson City *above* stands on a bluff overlooking the Missouri River. On the river bank can be seen the 'Signing of the Treaty' *below*, a memorial depicting the signing of the Louisiana Purchase, by Monroe, Livingston and Marbois. Symbolic of St. Louis, Eero Saarinen's awe-inspiring stainless steel 'Gateway Arch' *left and center right*, soaring 630 feet high, dominates the Jefferson National Expansion Memorial. Miles Fountain *bottom right*, with its sculptured group of fourteen bronze figures denoting the 'Wedding of the Waters' of the Missouri and Mississippi Rivers is one of St. Louis' loveliest fountains. The University of Missouri, Colombia, the oldest west of the Mississippi, is shown *top right*, and *overleaf* the glittering skyline of Kansas City.

183

Along the waterfront of St. Louis *above left*, where riverboats such as the Robert E. Lee, *right*, still ply the Mississippi, the monument *below*, at Laclede's Landing is sited in the last remaining historic site of the area, while the panorama of downtown St. Louis *above*, seen from 'Gateway Arch', reveals the splendid Old Court House set amid the gleaming skyscrapers. Pictured *left* is the Country Club Christian Church at Kansas, Missouri.

THIS MONUMENT
IS ERECTED
TO COMMEMORATE
THE LANDING OF THE
FOUNDERS OF THE
CITY OF SAINT LOUIS
PIERRE LIGUEST LACLEDE
AND COMPANIONS IN
THE YEAR 1764

ERECTED BY SAINT LOUIS
GENERAL ASSEMBLY
FOURTH DEGREE
KNIGHTS OF COLUMBUS
OCTOBER 12. 1923

The old Conestoga wagon *above left* at Scott's
Bluff is reminiscent of the early pioneer days
when the wagons would roll across the dusty
overland trail of Nebraska. In Scouts Rest
Ranch Historical State Park, North Platte,
stands the home *left* of one of the era's most
colorful figures, 'Buffalo Bill' Cody, who
popularized American history in his spectacular
Wild West shows. Little Missouri River *above*
and the Cannon Ball Concretions *right* are part
of the vast Theodore Roosevelt National
Memorial Park in the Badlands of North
Dakota. In Bismarck, the state's capital, rises
the 'skyscraper of the prairies' – the white
limestone State Capitol Building *below*. On the
granite face of Mount Rushmore, South
Dakota *overleaf*, are carved the colossal heads of
four of the nation's greatest leaders:
Washington, Jefferson, Lincoln and Roosevelt.

Phoenix *below*, situated on the Salt River on a prehistoric site first occupied by the Hohokam Indians, is Arizona's thriving and vital capital. The neo-classical State Capitol *top left*, built of native tufa and granite, contains several important murals, while in the newly completed Civic Plaza, a six-square-block convention center, can be seen John Vaddell's sculpture group 'the Dancers' *center left*, and St. Mary's church *right* beyond the fountain which contains a contemporary interpretation of the legendary 'Phoenix Bird Ascending'. Often referred to as the 'White Dove of the Desert', the beautiful Mission San Xavier del Sac *bottom left*, is located southwest of Tucson, the Civic Centre of which is shown *above*.

194

Once spanning the River Thames, London Bridge *top left*, brought brick by brick from England and reassembled over a man-made channel of the Colorado River, in the Arizona desert, is set in a popular resort complex *this page* at Lake Havasu.

Erected in 1940 by Columbia Pictures, Old Tucson *top far right* has served as a location for the movie ''Arizona'' and the television series ''High Chaparral''.

Tombstone *far center right* and *below far right* is famous as the notorious old Arizona mining town which was dubbed ''the Town too Tough to Die''. In 1877 the prospector Ed Schieffelin struck his first gold in the area, and because he had been told by the Fort Huachuca soldiers that he would find only his tombstone there, applied the name to his first claim, which was adopted by the settlement as it developed into a boom town. Boothill Graveyard *center right* and *right*, containing the graves of 180 infamous characters, who met their untimely ends in common with the 'claim jumper' *top right*, is located at the north city limits.

From the majestic peaks of Hopi Point *above and previous page*, Mohave Point *right* and Moran Point *left*, the muted splendor of the Grand Canyon's south rim fans out to meet the horizon. Layer upon layer of stratified rock rises from the canyon floor, where the Colorado River, seen at Lee's Ferry *below* winds like a slender blue ribbon in one of the world's most awe-inspiring natural spectacles.

Fields of alfalfa at Parker *top right* are watered
by the essential irrigation system that is
provided by a series of dams throughout
Arizona that have been one of the state's most
extensive projects. In the Glen Canyon
National Recreation Area, encompassing Lake
Powell, is located Glen Canyon Dam *center
left*, the fourth highest in the United States,
while Hoover Dam, seen across Black Canyon
bottom left, and, at 726 feet high, one of the
highest dams ever constructed, impounds one
of the world's largest artificial lakes, the vast
Lake Mead. East of the Apache Trail, which
was built in 1905 to transport supplies from
Phoenix and Globe for the construction of the
Roosevelt Dam *above left*, are the brooding
Superstition Mountains *below right*, so named
for the many legends surrounding them.

Reflecting the sun's warm rays, brilliantly
colored rock formations such as Cathedral
Rock at Red Rock Crossing in Sedona's Oak
Creek Canyon *above*, and the East and West
Mittens with Merrick Butte in Monument
Valley, Navajo Trail Park *overleaf*, are a
fascinating aspect of the Arizona Desert.
Montezuma Castle, a 20-roomed prehistoric
cliff dwelling which is one of the best
preserved of its kind, is shown *below*.

Arizona's monuments rank among the most magnificent in the country and their incredible diversity is evidenced in: Canyon de Chelly *left*, which displays five periods of Indian culture; Little Colorado River Gorge near Gray Mountain *above*; the vividly colored Painted Desert *above right* and *bottom*, and majestic Monument Valley *overleaf*.

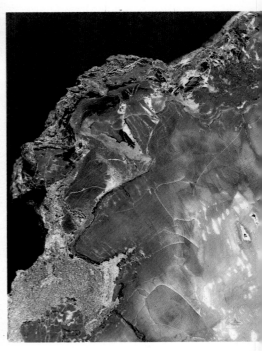

The Petrified Forest National Park *bottom left* displays an abundance of petrified coniferous trees, a fragment of which is shown *above*, as well as numerous fossil plants and bones. Heavy concentrations of petrified wood are to be found in five areas of the park, including the Blue Mesa *center left* and *below right*.

Exotic cacti, such as the prickly pear, with its bright, golden flowers *top left*, and the vermilion tinged hedgehog *bottom left*, bring life and color to the arid Arizona deserts. Rare cacti, like the organ pipe, a close-up of which is shown *below*, are preserved in Organ Pipe National Monument, where the giant Saguaro *above* is silhouetted against a dramatic sunset.

The Saguaro National Monument *center left*, contains dense stands of Saguaro cactus which can live up to 200 years, reaching heights of 25 to 36 feet and, in exceptional cases can even exceed 50 feet. Against a cloudless sky the giant specimen *right* stands like a sentinel near Apache Junction, while the golden barrel cactus *below* can provide a useful source of water in emergencies.

Taos, exuding a delightful Spanish atmosphere is a picturesque New Mexico city which contains the highest pueblo buildings in the Southwest. In the Pueblo, with its graceful church *top left*, are the terraced communal dwellings and flat-topped adobe houses *above*, which still provide accommodation for about 400 Indians. Mission of San Miguel *bottom left*, one of the oldest churches in the country, and the First Presbyterian Church *below*, are located in New Mexico's charming capital Santa Fe. Sited 25 miles southeast of the capital is Pecos National Monument, the impressive ruins of which can be seen *center left*, while *below right* is shown the Fort Union National Monument.

In the downtown area of New Albuquerque, seen from the Sheraton Old Town Inn *top left*, the modern skyscrapers are in direct contrast to the historic Old Town which, since its foundation over 250 years ago by the Duke of Albuquerque has retained the characteristic Spanish flavor of those early 18th century days. One of the Old Town's most interesting buildings is the San Felipe de Neri Church *right*, sited on the northwest corner of the Plaza, and although remodeled and enlarged on several occasions, reveals its basic adobe architecture beneath a solid Victorian overlay. The Indian Pueblo Cultural Center, where the dancers *above* perform, is constructed in the style of the Pueblo Bonito in Chaco Canyon and provides a fascinating insight into the history and culture of the Pueblo Indians.

Coursing south through the center of New Mexico, the mighty Rio Grande is shown *center left*, near Taos; *bottom left* can be seen the State Capitol in Sante Fe, and pictured *below and bottom* are Indian children at play in Red Rocks State Park.

Covering almost 300 square miles, the dazzling white gypsum sands of New Mexico's White Sands National Monument *above right* shimmer like a sea of alabaster.

Santuario de Chimayo *left, above and below,* drawing many pilgrims to its shrine for the curative earth found in a pit inside the chapel, is built, according to legend, on the site of the martyrdom of two priests. Aloof and gaunt, the massive peak of Shiprock *right* is sharply outlined against a glowing sunset.

Formed in a limestone reef by percolating ground water, the vast underground chambers of the Carlsbad Caverns *these pages*, are situated beneath the rugged foothills of the Guadalupe Mountains. In this subterranean wonderland, the huge galleries are filled with delicate stone formations, massive stalactites and stalagmites which, tinted by the minerals and iron in the limestone, produce a fascinating, iridescent glow.

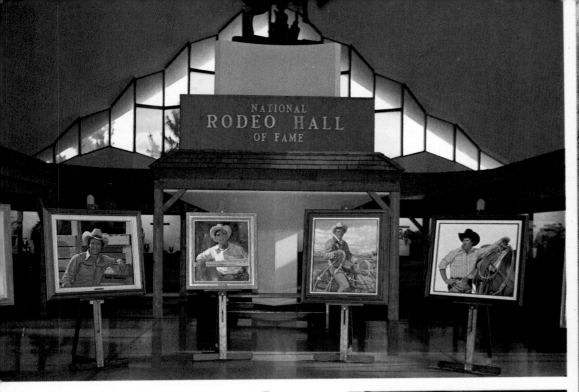

Oklahoma City *right*, with its beautiful State Capitol Building *bottom left* is noted as the location of two of the largest high gravity oilfields in the world. Among the state capital's many interesting museums is the National Cowboy Hall of Fame *top left*, which contains a wealth of exhibits, including the sculptures *center left and below*, dedicated to the men and women who made significant contributions to the development of the West.

Set in lush Italianate gardens is Tulsa's exquisite Philbrook Art Center *above*.

219

Austin, built on a series of hills flanking the Colorado River, was the first American settlement in Texas and was named for its founder, Stephen F. Austin. Seen from Congress Avenue *left*, the pink granite building of the State Capitol *above right* was completed in 1888, while *right* is shown the superb stadium of the University of Texas. The thriving metropolis of Dallas, with its sleek skyscrapers *above* and communications Tower *below*, is the state's second largest city.

21

Since John Neeley Bryan built his cabin – now sited at the corner of Market and Elm Streets *right* – on the banks of the Upper Trinity River, in 1841, the city of Dallas has grown progressively, to become the Southwest's largest banking center, a leader in wholesale business and a dynamic communications and transport hub. The soaring glass office buildings *left and above*, intermingled with graceful plazas, are part of this well-planned metropolis where towering skyscrapers are contrasted with gracious suburbs and tranquil green parks. Designed as a place of meditation, the simplistic memorial *below* was erected by the people of Dallas in honor of President John F. Kennedy, who was assassinated here in 1963.

223

A golden sunset floods the skyline of Houston *above right*, this vibrant Texas metropolis which ranks among the country's greatest seaports. Transformed at night by a million glittering lights *above*, the sleek lines of the skyscrapers can be seen by day *below right* across tranquil Sam Houston Park, while Freeway 59 *left* is part of Houston's elaborate road system *below* which curves round the city.

In addition to being a highly successful industrial center, Houston is also noted for its cultural and recreational facilities and boasts over eight institutions, including the important Rice University *top left*. *Center left and above* is shown the popular amusement park of Astroworld, which provides over 100 rides, attractions, liveshows and shops.

Right can be seen the ice-rink within the Galleria, a multi-story shopping, office and entertainment complex; *bottom left* colorfully costumed Indians on the Alabama-Coushatta Reservation which is located in the heart of Sam-Houston National Forest; *below* the U.S.S. Texas, only survivor of the Dreadnought Class – moored at San Jacinto since 1948, and *above* the exterior of the Summit Stadium where star-spangled banners flutter proudly in the breeze.

The magnificent Harris County Domed Stadium, known as the Astrodome *these pages*, is the world's first enclosed, air-conditioned major league baseball stadium. Standing on a 260-acre site the stadium has a plush seating capacity for up to 66,000 people and boasts the world's largest electronic scoreboard.

Home of the Houston Astro's, the team is featured on *these pages* in a stimulating game against the Giants.

The NASA Lyndon B. Johnson Space Center *above* is situated near Clear Lake on a 1,620 acre site and consists of about 100 different buildings, including the nine story Project Management Building *below*. One of the newest and largest research and development facilities, the center is a focal point of the Nation's manned space flight program. Among the exhibits on view to the public are the Apollo 17 Command Module *far right*; the Travehicular Mobility Unit *right*; the Lunar Module Test Article *left* and the flight articles *above left*.

231

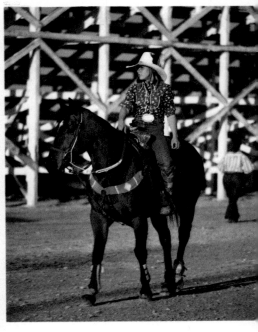

Texas has long been famous for its cattle industry and, although the longhorn *center left* has been usurped by other breeds, Texas beef and dairy cattle still play an important part in the state's economy. Shown *top and top left* is an auction at Amarillo *right*, and *bottom left*, *above and below*, the Pecos Rodeo.

Extending some 750 miles in length and breadth, the huge Texas landscape displays a magnificent variety of scenery, seen in Pulliam Ridge, at the edge of the Chisos Basin *top left*; the Rio Grande as it tumbles into the international waters of Lake Amistad *bottom left*; and the undulating Monahans sandhills *below*, while in its well-planned cities, modern structures, such as those in the lovely El Paso Civic Center, *center left*, and traditional Spanish Colonial buildings like San Antonio's Landmark Building *above*, blend harmoniously with historic monuments such as Mission San Antonio de Valero *right and top*, better known as the famous Alamo.

234

Known as the 'Mile High City', Denver, Colorado's cosmopolitan capital, is the cultural and commercial center of the Rocky Mountain area. Its majestic, gold-domed State Capitol *above and below*, built of Colorado granite, was constructed between 1887 and 1895. Overlooking Denver, at the top of Lookout Mountain, is the grave *top left*, of W. F. Cody, the famous 'Buffalo Bill'.

Silverton, once a booming mining town in the San Juan mountain district, is today a popular tourist attraction and during the summer months visitors can take advantage of the narrow gauge passenger train *bottom left* which operates between the towns of Silverton and Durango.

Central City, an old mining town established during the boom of the 1800's, is shown *below right*, and *center left* is the fabulous ski center of Steamboat, at Steamboat Springs.

Mountain lakes and resorts, trout streams and eleven magnificent national forests are part of the vast recreational area in Colorado's beautiful Rocky Mountains. The majestic splendor of tranquil mirror lakes, set like jewels amid the thickly-forested mountain slopes is evidenced in Bear Lake, in the Rocky Mountain National Park *above right*; Dream Lake, reflecting Hallett Peak and Flat Top Mountain *below right*, and Beaver Ponds in Hidden Valley *overleaf*.

Rolling countryside backed by tiers of aspen, seen at Doyleville in Gunnison County *above*, gives way to sparkling rivers like those of Cimarron *top left*, bordered by russet-leaved trees, and Crystal *center left* as it courses through the Gunnison National Forests near Marble; while *bottom left* the swirling waters bubble across the boulder-strewn bed of Maroon Creek.

In the Black Canyon of the Gunnison *below*, the somber-colored spires of granite rise from the floor of the gorge, where the winding river has cut into some of the earth's oldest base rocks.

In Georgetown, the 'Silver Queen of the Rockies', the carefully preserved Victorian buildings such as the Bowman/White House *top right*, perpetuate an aura of history which recalls its early days as a thriving silver mining center. One of the town's most famous buildings is the Hotel de Paris, established in 1875 by Louis du Puy and which today still retains much of the authentic furnishings, as the dining room *center right* and kitchen *bottom right*, with its antique stove and accessories, shows. Connecting the communities of Georgetown and Silver Plume, the Georgetown Loop Railroad *above left*, features a steam locomotive which tours the original mining area.

Against a mountain backdrop *above*, the seventeen spires of Colorado's Air Force Academy Cadet Chapel soar to a height of 150 feet. Designed to meet the spiritual needs of cadets, the glass, aluminium and steel structure contains three separate chapels, one for each of the major religious faiths.

Dedicated to the memory of Will Rogers, the Shrine of the Sun *below*, an imposing fortress-tower built of local grey-pink granite, is located high on the slopes of Cheyenne Mountain.

In fall, the leaves of the silver-barked aspen trees *below left*, flood the Colorado landscape with rich hues.

Ramshackle cabins nestling amid Colorado's pine-clad mountain slopes are poignant reminders of those days when eager prospectors, drawn by stories of rich gold and silver strikes, would flock to the mountains in the hope of making their fortunes. Dilapidated Deadhorse Mill *left* teeters on its rocky bank in the Crystal area, and *right* can be seen the old ghost town of Sneffels, near Ouray. Beyond majestic Maroon Lake *above*, the thickly-carpeted slopes, studded with trees, rise in steps from the water's edge.

Fascinating cliff-dwellings like Cliff Palace *below*, created by the early Pueblo Indians, can be seen in the Mesa Verde, one of the nation's major archaeological preserves.

Jagged mountain peaks, seen in the Sawtooth Mountains as they rise behind tranquil Redfish Lake *above*, and cascading streams *right*, express the rugged beauty of Idaho, where spectacular mountain groups and vast lava plains are contrasted with numerous lakes and copious wheatfields. Glowing basalt columns, rich in iron and magnesium are shown *left*, above Morse Creek, and *below* the incredible Balanced Rock, located near Twin Falls.

46

Glacier National Park, in scenic Montana, containing some of the country's finest mountain scenery, as seen in Mount Reynolds near Logan Pass *right*, is also a noted wildlife preserve. Its spectacular lakes, most of which are of glacial origin, number 200, and include Hidden Lake at Logan Pass *left* and Iceberg Lake in the Many Glacier Region *above*; while *below* the unusual rock formations reveal the dramatic beauty of Montana's isolated mountain groups.

The Prince of Wales Hotel, set amid the splendor of Waterton Lakes National Park *overleaf*, provides an idyllic retreat in its perfect setting.

Reno *below left* and Las Vegas *these pages*, Nevada's fun-loving cities, glitter and sparkle twenty-four hours a day with a wealth of gambling casinos such as the Golden Nugget *center right*, and fabulous entertainments that draw millions of visitors annually to these internationally famous resorts.

From Las Vegas visitors can embark on a scenic helicopter ride over Hoover Dam *above left*, the Grand Canyon and Colorado River.

Spectacular entertainment and plush gambling halls are a particular feature of the glamorous Las Vegas and Reno hotels. Harrah's Hotel in Reno is shown *below*; Del Webb's Sahara Tahoe, Reno *above right*; the Folies Bergere at the Tropicana Hotel, Las Vegas, *right*; and *above* and *left* 'Hello Hollywood' – an award-winning musical extravaganza at the MGM Grand Hotel, Las Vegas.

255

Sliced by the Angel River, Zion Canyon, in Zion National Park, is a spectacular multi-colored gorge, where gigantic stone masses such as 'The Watchman' *top left*; 'Lady Mountain' *center left*; 'The Towers of the Virgin' *bottom left*; 'The Sentinel' *below*; 'The Court of the Patriarchs' *above*, and the 'East Temple' *right* dominate the landscape in Utah's dramatic desert and canyon country. Intricately sculpted formations in the horseshoe-shaped amphitheater of Bryce Canyon are pictured *overleaf.*

At Lower Falls, in the Grand Canyon of Yellowstone *overleaf*, the tumbling river cascades to the depths of the gorge and snakes its way between the brilliantly colored rocks *left* in this spectacular area of Wyoming's renowned Yellowstone National Park. Old Faithful *above* is one of about 10,000 geysers and hot springs in the park's fascinating geyser basins. The snow-covered slopes of Medicine Bow Mountains *below*, in the Medicine Bow National Forest, are regally reflected in the mirror waters of Lake Marie *top right*. In Bridger Wilderness, a vast expanse of scenic mountain country in the Bridger-Teton National Forest, the Green River Lakes *center right* are set like aquamarines amid the pine-clad mountains, while *bottom right* is shown the rugged splendor of the snow-powdered Teton Mountains.

In a little over a hundred years Balboa Park has been transformed from a wilderness into a center of cultural and recreational facilities for San Diego, in California. It now contains carefully landscaped gardens, art galleries, museums, theaters, a golf course and the world's largest zoo. The park was chosen as the site for the Panama-California International Exposition which was held in 1915 and 1916, after which it was given its present name. It was at this time that several of the beautiful exhibit halls were built in Spanish colonial style, including the lovely Casa del Prado *top and bottom left and below*, the California Tower *above*, and the Natural History Museum *center left*. Balboa Park was also the setting for another world's fair, the California-Pacific International Exposition which was staged in 1935 and 1936, when new exhibit halls, comprising the Pan-American Plaza, were built.

Standing tranquil and timeless in the California sunshine, Mission San Diego *right*, was founded by Juniper Serra and is known as the 'Mother of the Missions'.

Overleaf is pictured the Charthouse Golf Course and the San Diego-Coronado Bay Bridge, and on the following two pages is shown the beautifully landscaped Walter Annenberg Estate.

264

Los Angeles City Hall, once the tallest building in Southern California, can be seen *left* behind the peacock fountain and *below* in the background of the Civic Center Mall. The city's many outstanding architectural designs include the new Los Angeles County Art Museum *above*, which is ringed by magnificent reflecting pools, and the Century Plaza and Schubert Theater *right*.

Fabulous Beverley Hills is pictured *overleaf* with it's magnificent Plaza a mass of colorful blooms.

271

Long Beach is the home of the famous ocean liner 'Queen Mary', *center left* who made her final voyage in December 1967 and is now preserved as a museum, and equally fascinating is Los Angeles' Chinatown, part of which is shown *bottom left*.

In the heart of movietown, on Hollywood and Vine, stands the Capitol Records Building *bottom*, its famous 92-foot phonograph needle pointing skywards. The charming City Hall of Pasadena, which lies eleven miles northwest of the downtown district of Los Angeles, is pictured *below*.

274

Universal City Studios are the largest motion picture studios in the world, covering 420-acres. Founded in 1912, the studios contain a variety of sets such as that *above*, as well as the shark from 'Jaws' *top far left and top center*.

Watts Tower *below* is a unique memorial to Simon Rodia, an Italian immigrant who expressed a desire to 'leave something behind in his adopted country'. The towers were erected from various items of scrap and took 33 years to build, being completed in 1954.

Santa Anita Racetrack in Arcadia *right* boasts the largest annual purse distribution of any racecourse in the world, and *overleaf* is the equally famous Malibu Beach, noted for its movie colony.

Recreated in the style of a Roman villa, the J. Paul Getty Museum *below right* contains an outstanding collection of Greek and Roman antiquities, paintings and furnishings.

Scotty's Castle *right* is situated in California's Death Valley and is a blend of Moorish, Spanish, Italian and California Mission architecture. Santa Barbara retains the traditions of 'Old Spain' and is particularly noted for its magnificent Court House *left*, resembling a Spanish-Moorish castle.

Sited on the Carmel-Monterey peninsula is the lovely Mission of San Carlos Borromeo de Carmelo *above*, while *below* is shown one of the ornate pools in the grounds of the fabled William Randolph Hearst mansion high above San Simeon.

Overleaf is pictured one of the world's highest highway bridges, Bixby Creek, on Highway 1.

California's magnificent rugged coastline is particularly evident along Big Sur in Monterey County, seen *above* as the daytime mist hazes the horizon and *above right* as the setting sun casts a shimmer over the ocean's waves. Within the Pebble Beach area of the Monterey Peninsula the famous Pebble Beach Golf Course provides golfers with an exciting and challenging course, particularly at the 7th hole *right*. One of the most spectacular scenic routes in Monterey is along the 17-Mile Drive which also penetrates the pine woods of the Del Monte Forest. The view *left* shows the Lone Pine as the Drive curves along the rocky stretch of coast.

Pigeon Point Lighthouse, sited along the coast between Monterey and San Francisco, is shown *below* dramatically silhouetted against a golden sunset.

Water on three sides and, therefore, a degree of inaccessibility, has made San Francisco *previous pages*, conspicuously different from most other cities. Even the most recently constructed buildings such as Transamerica's pyramidal 'skysaver' *left* and, of course, the city's famous Chinatown *above right and overleaf* have their own distinctive character. One of San Francisco's 'rolling symbols' – a cablecar – is shown *below*, and *above* is a view of the famous Fisherman's Wharf.

The tallest and largest single span suspension bridge in the world, with a 90-foot wide traffic deck and two pedestrian walks, the Golden Gate Bridge *right* spans the historic Golden Gate of San Francisco and remains the single most lasting and impressive symbol of this most beautiful city.

287

High in the Sierra Nevada, in remote splendor, is Silver Lake *top left*.

Yosemite National Park comprises almost 1,200 miles of varied scenery and breathtaking beauty. It was created, principally, when huge blocks of granite, formed beneath the earth's surface, were buckled and lifted by immense pressure. This was followed by glacial action of a more recent date which continued nature's handiwork by carving huge valleys and basins, which eventually became lakes.

Waterfalls tumble down granite rock faces and the peaks are sculpted into fantastic and strangely beautiful shapes. Wild flowers and wildlife abound in the area's many acres of pine, fir and oak forest.

Fall adds the magic of its own coloring to the park's trees *above* and the Merced River *right* threads its way along the floor of the Yosemite Valley, passing, on its way, such towering cliffs as El Capitan *below* and the mist-shrouded and mysterious-seeming Cathedral Spires *left*.

292

Oregon, a state of immense wealth and beauty, is unsurpassed in its variety of landscapes, lavish scenery and superb, unspoilt ocean beaches *center left*. In the major Cascade Range, dividing the state into two distinct regions, the volcanic peaks of the perpetually snow-clad Mount Hood *above*, Mount Jefferson *top left* and the Three Sisters Mountains *bottom left*, tower above the surrounding mountains. They were created by the same lava flow which formed the central and southeastern plateau. It was the eruption and collapse of the stratovolcano, Mazama, that created the setting for the beautiful, jewel-like Crater Lake *previous page*.

Amid the winding paths in the Oregon Cascades, misty falls, such as Ramona *right* and the Lower Proxy Falls *overleaf*, tumble down moss-covered rock in the majestic alpine range which, with its isolated wilderness areas provides a perfect vacationland for hikers and horseback riders.

Perched on a splendid headland overlooking the restless Pacific surf is the picturesque Heceta Head lighthouse *below*.

Snow-capped Mount Baker *left* in the majestic North Cascades *right*; the brooding north side of Willis Wall in Mount Rainier National Park *above*; the beautiful lake in Olympic National Park *below* and the lush, rolling countryside *overleaf* reveal the varied beauty of Washington's National Parks.

Superb ocean beaches like Ilwaco *above* and fertile valleys where carpets of tulips bloom *left* are contrasted with the rugged splendor of Washington's National Parks. *Above right* can be seen the Sol Duc Falls in Olympic National Park; *below* the Comet Falls in Mount Rainier National Park, and *right* the tropical rain forest in Olympic National Forest.

Waikiki Beach, in Hawaii *left and above*, is a renowned resort and justifiably a favorite with vacationers. The long, sandy beach is now backed by a considerable number of modern hotels, and fishing, scuba-diving, snorkeling and surfing are just a few of the many pursuits that can be enjoyed here.

Part of Waikiki is shown *top right* across Ala Wai harbor, with a threatening sky as a backdrop, and *bottom right* is St. Peter's Catholic Church, which was built on the site of an ancient Hawaiian temple.

Brightly colored dresses, leis, palm trees and the inevitable guitars *center right*, delight the many visitors who enjoy the spectacle offered by the Kodak Hawaii Hula Show at the Waikiki Shell.

A young Hawaiian couple *below* sample the pleasures and beauty of Coco Palms Lagoon in an outrigger canoe, surely an ideal method of transport, and the unforgettable sight of a sunset in Hawaii is pictured *overleaf* on the coast of West Maui.

Top left is featured the drama, thrill and skill of surfing, and *below* a beautiful Hawaiian girl named Noelaui is shown with one of her marine friends in Sea Life Park on Oahu Island.

Devastation Trail *top right*, is a half-mile boardwalk that provides a path through a volcanic area of pumice, cinders and lifeless trees, and *above* is Kalalau Valley, an area of spectacular beauty.

A rainbow adds a further touch of color to the sky behind Makuaikaua Church and Hulihee Palace *left*, while sailing boats drift gently at their moorings in Lahaina Harbor *center right*. The remarkable Fern Grotto near Wailua is shown *below*, and *right* anthuriums flower in the shade of ferns in the Puna district.

At Pearl Harbor *overleaf* is the Arizona Memorial, which honors the many sailors who were lost when, in 1941, the battleship Arizona was sunk.

309

Alaska, the vast 'winter wonderland', called *Alashka* or 'Great Land' by the Aleuts, is a country of vivid contrasts, evidenced in its glaciers, tundra, snow-peaked mountains such as the Alaska range *overleaf*, fishing and wildlife, permafrost, fiords and Eskimo villages. For centuries the remarkable Eskimo people *above* have made their homes in the barren wastes and harsh climate of the far north and western Arctic coastline, where the musher and dog team *below* cross the frozen Bering Sea.

In the fishing country around Homer Spit, where small boats lie becalmed in the ice-encrusted harbor *top left*, commercial fishing boats bring home their catches of salmon, halibut, shrimp and king crab; while Valdez, ringed by snow-capped mountains, is the state's northernmost ice-free port and, with its picturesque small boat harbor *center left* and alpine houses *below right* is justifiably known as the 'Switzerland of Alaska'. Nome, once a gold-rush camp which housed thousands during the late 19th century, is shown *bottom left*, and *above right* is the famous ski area of Alyeska, south of Anchorage.

In the remote region of the Bering Sea Coast, where the satellite station *center left* is located, the vast barren landscape, devoid of trees, stretches northwards toward the Arctic Circle. Here, during the winter, in seacoast cities like Nome, the frozen ocean crusted with frosty peaks, seen at Norton Sound *right*, becomes a huge extension of the land and Eskimos travel on the hard-packed surface by snowmobile, or by dog sled, pulled by huskies *above*, over the frozen Bering Sea *top left*. The monument *below*, on the Richardson Highway, commemorates the country's first great road . builder, the U.S. Army General, Wilds P. Richardson.

Along the Sterling Highway, the unmarked snow, pierced by stark remnants of summer's flora, stretches far into the horizon and merges with an inky sky *left*, while at Mineral Creek, just outside Valdez *right*, the ice-encrusted terrain is backed by jagged mountain peaks, the slopes thickly powdered by the winter snow.

Beyond the airport at the native village of Gulkana, rises snow-clad Mount Drum *below*, one of the majestic peaks in the Wrangell Mountains.

A musher and dog team drive over the frozen Bering Sea as warm sunshine whitens the driven snow *left*, and *right* as lengthening shadows mark the close of day, while *above* a full moon glows over the deepening blue landscape on the Iditarod Trail at Nome, marking the end of the famous 1,000-mile Sled Dog Race which starts from Anchorage on the first Saturday in March. *Top right and below* can be seen the famed Portage Glacier in the Chugach National Forest, the nation's second largest, and *center right* the shimmering Northern Lights over the log cabins at Summit Lake.

First published in 1979 by Colour Library International Ltd.
© 1979 Illustrations and text: Colour Library International Ltd., 163 East 64th St., New York, N.Y. 10021.
Colour separations by FERCROM, Barcelona, Spain.
Display and text filmsetting by Focus Photoset, London, England.
Printed and bound by JISA-RIEUSSET, Barcelona, Spain.
ISBN 0-8317-9084-9 Library of Congress Catalogue Card No. 79-90610
Published in the United States of America by Mayflower Books, Inc., New York City

D.L. B-8.150-81

WE HOLD THESE TRUTHS TO BE SELF-EVIDENT: THAT ALL MEN ARE CREATED EQUAL, THAT THEY ARE ENDOWED BY THEIR CREATOR WITH CERTAIN INALIENABLE RIGHTS, AMONG THESE ARE LIFE, LIBERTY AND THE PURSUIT OF HAPPINESS, THAT TO SECURE THESE RIGHTS GOVERNMENTS ARE INSTITUTED AMONG MEN. WE... SOLEMNLY PUBLISH AND DECLARE, THAT THESE COLONIES ARE AND OF RIGHT OUGHT TO BE FREE AND INDEPENDENT STATES...AND FOR THE SUPPORT OF THIS DECLARATION, WITH A FIRM RELIANCE ON THE PROTECTION OF DIVINE PROVIDENCE, WE MUTUALLY PLEDGE OUR LIVES, OUR FORTUNES AND OUR SACRED HONOUR.
THOMAS JEFFERSON
1743 – 1826